25 Myths About Bullying and Cyberbullying

Elizabeth K. Englander

WILEY Blackwell

This edition first published 2020
© 2020 John Wiley & Sons, Inc.

The right of Elizabeth K. Englander to be identified as the author of this work has been asserted in accordance with law.

Registered Office
John Wiley & Sons, Inc., 111 River Street, Hoboken, NJ 07030, USA

Editorial Office
111 River Street, Hoboken, NJ 07030, USA

For details of our global editorial offices, customer services, and more information about Wiley products visit us at www.wiley.com.

Wiley also publishes its books in a variety of electronic formats and by print-on-demand. Some content that appears in standard print versions of this book may not be available in other formats.

Library of Congress Cataloging-in-Publication Data
Names: Englander, Elizabeth Kandel, author.
Title: 25 myths about bullying and cyberbullying / Elizabeth K. Englander.
Other titles: Twenty-five myths about bullying and cyberbullying
Description: Hoboken, NJ: Wiley Blackwell, 2020. | Includes
    bibliographical references and index.
Identifiers: LCCN 2019052193 (print) | LCCN 2019052194 (ebook) | ISBN
    9781118736500 (paperback) | ISBN 9781118736708 (adobe pdf) | ISBN
    9781118736562 (epub)
Subjects: LCSH: Bullying. | Cyberbullying.
Classification: LCC BF637.B85 E54 2020 (print) | LCC BF637.B85 (ebook) |
    DDC 302.34/3–dc23
LC record available at https://lccn.loc.gov/2019052193
LC ebook record available at https://lccn.loc.gov/2019052194

Cover Design: Wiley
Cover Image: © Erin Lester/Getty Images

Set in 11.5/14pt STIXTwoText by SPi Global, Pondicherry, India

Printed in the United States of America

V10017758_022720

25 Myths About Bullying and Cyberbullying

Contents

About the Author

Dr. Elizabeth K. Englander is the founder and executive director of the Massachusetts Aggression Reduction Center (*MARC*) at Bridgewater State University, delivering programs, resources, and research to more than 400 schools every year nationwide. As a researcher and a professor of psychology for 25 years, she is a nationally recognized expert in the areas of bullying and cyberbullying, childhood causes of aggression and abuse, and children's use of social media and technology. She was named Most Valuable Educator of 2013 by the Boston Red Sox because of her work in technological aggression and how it interacts with peer abusiveness in general. In 2018, she was appointed to the Massachusetts Governor's Juvenile Justice Advisory Council. Dr. Englander is also the chair of the Cyberbullying Workgroup for the Institute of Child Development and Digital Media. Each year, Dr. Englander trains and supervises graduate and undergraduate students and collaborates with multiple agencies around the state of Massachusetts and across the nation.

Preface

Have you ever heard of the Momo Challenge?

If you're lucky enough to have missed it, the *Momo Challenge* was a widely hyped Internet panic. The idea was that an intensely scary character could, unprovoked, pop up on the screen while any child was using any website and urge that user to hurt themselves. The chatter was frightening, but once you stepped back, the assumptions were a little bizarre: sure, maybe the scary character could pop up on any website; but could it really be true that even a healthy, well-adjusted child could take the "challenge" and end up committing suicide?

Despite some media reports that purported to demonstrate the allegedly incredible power of this challenge through real-life examples, it was never verified. A few cases that initially depicted Momo Challenge suicides seemed to have other, more plausible explanations; and in any case, they were far from widespread. Many reports came from social media instead of mainstream news media. The Momo Challenge may have been a hoax, or it may have been true but far less scary or widespread than it was depicted as being.

But the damage that Internet scares can do was already done. The Momo Challenge – true or false – became yet another incident in modern life seemingly designed to scare parents out of their wits.

For all our modern conveniences, it's not an easy time to be a parent. We have age-old problems on a new scale, like bullying. We also have entirely new problems for which we have no history to use as a guide, like cyberbullying (and Internet scares). Parents today aren't indifferent or uncaring; yet when it comes to our efforts to reduce bullying and cyberbullying, it sometimes feels like a case of two steps forward, one step back. We've made some progress in reducing bullying and cyberbullying, but in doing so we've also created other problems. At times, you may feel like you're so focused on protecting your children that they're not able to have a "normal" childhood. Technological innovations have also introduced new complications into the mix – most notably, digital communications and the use of social media. Children today grow up very differently from past generations.

But while these are challenging times, human beings have a pretty good track record when it comes to addressing stubborn problems. Consider: in the last few decades, we've successfully reduced teenage pregnancy, violent crime, illiteracy, school drop-outs, and many other trials in the developed world. Like these, aggression and bullying are stubborn problems; but don't mistake this statement for fatalism. We can improve these troubles as well. The fact is, we've already made some solid progress. Many of us now recognize how serious a problem bullying and cyberbullying can be.

So, why did I write this book? Some of the ways we've addressed bullying and cyberbullying can actually hamper us if we're not careful. While our focus on bullying and cyberbullying has undoubtedly helped children become healthier and less aggressive, that focus has also resulted in a lot of noise, misinformation, myths, and anxiety for parents and children. This book addresses that noise and misinformation. These myths are not only ineffective; they can actively impede our efforts to reduce bullying and cyberbullying. This book is designed to help parents reject myths and become more effective in helping to guide our kids through modern childhood and adolescence.

As with my other books, it took a village to produce this one. I have a great deal of help and support, from my editors at Wiley to my staff at the Massachusetts Aggression Reduction Center and at Bridgewater State University. Special thanks to Jayne Fargnoli and Melissa Duphily for your support. But the real wind beneath my wings comes from my children – Josh, Nick, and Max – and my steadfastly wonderful husband, Michael, who believes in me and never has a moment's doubt. Love to all of you.

Elizabeth K. Englander
Boston, Massachusetts
2020

Chapter 1
Why Talk About Myths Instead of Facts?

Maybe you're looking for a really satisfying story about bullying: perhaps a story about someone who was viciously bullied, but who stood up fearlessly and made the bully wither in public shame through the use of their razor-sharp wit; or who, surrounded by supportive and admiring friends, felt nothing but supremely self-confident indifference. Those are the stories we all want to hear and the stories we've all dreamed about, although as a teenager I personally only came up with cutting retorts hours or days too late. I think it's common to dream about heroic solutions to bullying; some things never change. On the other hand, certain things about bullying have definitely changed – a *lot*. Twenty years ago, we might have laughed if someone had suggested that by 2010, bullying by *girls* would be just as much of a public health concern as boys' aggression. Bullying in *suburban* schools as a major problem? Bullying in private schools? In religious and parochial schools? *Cyber*bullying?

25 Myths About Bullying and Cyberbullying, First Edition.
Elizabeth K. Englander.
© 2020 John Wiley & Sons, Inc. Published 2020 by John Wiley & Sons, Inc.

Maybe your kids have been bullied, or maybe you worry that they will be. Bullying today still happens, at times, in a more traditional way: for example, a little boy could be bullied on the playground by a slightly older boy. It can also happen in new and confounding ways: perhaps a teenage girl discovers that a topless photo, sent privately to a date, has been distributed around the school, and the result is a social crisis for her. What you read, see, and hear about bullying may feel familiar, or it may feel utterly alien. The fact is, bullying is a social problem that has remained the same, but it's also gone through a monumental metamorphosis. Back in the early 1990s, the violence-prevention focus was almost entirely on boys and gang violence, and with good reason: America was in the midst of a terrible violent crime wave, and Americans were enduring a daily onslaught of bad news about violent males. In 1995, a Princeton professor, John DiIulio, even coined the term *superpredator* to describe what he envisioned as a looming generation of totally callous and aggressive male criminals.[1] Few researchers, if any, anticipated the dramatic drop in traditional violent crime that was about to occur, or the emergence of bullying and cyberbullying as key concerns.

The result is that today, you can scarcely watch a newscast or read a newsfeed without seeing a story about bullying or cyberbullying. The troubles spattered across our media today aren't only new; they're newly confounding. Kids who bully a schoolmate who's disabled, mocking him or her. Schools that ban cell phones, only to find that kids continue to text each other on their Fitbits. New and baffling problems, articles, opinions, and advice abound. Yet even this large (indeed, sometimes overwhelming) flood of information doesn't provide many answers about what to believe (is cyberbullying really rampant?), how to tell when something is truly a problem (my son seems OK with the apparently abusive talk that takes place during online video games), or what parents are supposed to actually *do* (or *not* do, as the case may be). Should you try to force your reluctant child to talk about a bullying situation? Will taking away their cell phone make the situation worse or better? The schools say "Tell us everything," but your child begs for confidentiality – now what? How do you help your son or daughter learn to properly use digital devices when they're the expert and you're the pupil? How can you make your child less vulnerable – more self-confident, more popular? The school tells you that your child bullied someone, but your child says *they're* the victim. The other kid's parents say it was a fight. Now what?

Ironically, the high level of interest that surrounds these problems could easily raise the sneaking suspicion that bullying is just the currently fashionable psychobabble rather than a genuine predicament. There's a kernel of truth to that. It does seem as though the word *bullying* is applied to almost any situation where someone's feelings are hurt. In a 2018 study of more than 600 teens, I found that 62% of the kids who believed they were "bullied" were actually using the word to describe different problems, such as fights with friends. And like all fashionable disorders, bullying may be less common than we think. For a few years now, a number of surveys have found *reductions* in the rate of bullying, rather than increases. One study of 27 countries in Europe and North America found that most countries are reporting less bullying. England, Norway, Australia, Spain, and the United States have all found that traditional bullying is becoming less common. All this sounds like good news, yet these reassurances can still ring hollow. Even one case is too many if it's causing real misery, and statistics are cold comfort to those who suffer under bullying or who are forced to watch their children suffer.

Furthermore, regardless of the overall trends, contemporary forms of bullying and cyberbullying remain unsettling. You may have been left out of a party back in the third grade, but it's hard to imagine the impact on your daughter when a topless photo of her gets passed around an entire high school. One of the most difficult things about being a parent today isn't social cruelty per se, but the yawning gap in knowledge (particularly around digital issues) and a display of unmistakable human cruelty that is disquieting. Decreasing or increasing, the fact is that bullying and cyberbullying remain among the most commonly cited concerns expressed by parents and educators. A national poll of parents in 2017[2] found that bullying and cyberbullying were a number-one concern. Let's be clear: exaggerating dangers is destructive, since it can unnecessarily raise anxiety. But it's equally pointless to ignore real social problems, regardless of whether they are more common, less common, fundamentally new and different, or a rehashing of old conflicts and abuses. The key, I think, is figuring out how to separate the myths from the facts – and thereby identify the real problems.

Internationally, there's no paucity of efforts to prevent bullying and cyberbullying. Significant resources have been mobilized; and as of this writing, Canada, Britain, Australia, and almost every state in the United States have passed laws that seek to address these behaviors.[3] The European Commission has been working with social networking companies since 2009 to reduce online bullying risks. A casual search on the Internet reveals a veritable avalanche of resources to prevent bullying and cyberbullying – everything from Assertiveness Training to Zen Buddhism.

Yet even with all this attention, these difficulties stubbornly persist, in large part due to their fast-changing, emotional, and profoundly complex nature. The advice lags far behind the actual knowledge. Understanding what causes, stops, and is important about bullying and cyberbullying hasn't been made much easier by an Internet teeming with well-intentioned guidance. Googling the phrase "bullying because of a nude picture" in an attempt to help your teenage daughter cope yields a mind-bending 12.5 *million* websites. It's the largest library in the world, with heaps and piles of books stacked as high as a building but in no particular order. If you're looking for help with bullying and cyberbullying on the Internet, that's what you're up against. Sometimes new problems are difficult to handle because we don't have enough information; at other times they're difficult because we have *too much* information, and the information is hard to find, inaccessible, or the wrong type. The data are disorganized, and large segments are outdated. And not all bullying is alike. If you're looking for advice on how to handle bullying between middle school boys while playing a video game, you might find yourself reading recommendations about how to handle third-grade boys on the playground, or advice on how to avoid fights in the cafeteria between teenage boys.

Even if you do find information about exactly the type of issue you're concerned about, the sheer volume of opinions and advice can throw up yet another roadblock. Let's imagine a scenario in which your fourth-grade daughter is being targeted at school and online because she didn't invite a popular girl to her birthday party. Different sources of advice might offer wildly contradictory recommendations. Your daughter should tell school personnel so they can support her; or she should not tell, lest they decide she's a whiner and her friends label her a tattle. Her friends should stick by her, but maybe it's a friend who's targeting her. She should ignore the bully, or, alternatively, assertively tell the bully how she feels. How does she react online, and should that be different from how she responds at school? One resource may recommend keeping any messages or postings as evidence; another may suggest that they should be ignored and immediately deleted. And while traditionally most parents would go back to their own father or mother for parenting advice, you can't do that for these new types of problems. That means you've lost a major source of parenting support.

To make things more difficult, your own life experiences may also incline you to adopt solutions that may or may not work in this new and different environment. As an eight-year-old, you probably didn't have to deal with mean comments while playing an online game; but maybe you were in a playground bullying situation, and you hit the bully, who subsequently decided to leave you alone. Can these experiences help your child today? What happened to you was emotionally powerful – you remember it – but will that strategy still apply? It's not likely that any expert or school will recommend hitting back, but it's also undeniably true that *some* bullying situations involve an aggressor who seeks defenseless targets, and when they do hit back, that bully just might – maybe – pursue a different victim.

So maybe it worked for you. Will it work for your child? Even a cursory search will quickly show you that many experts – including myself – don't encourage this as a tactic that's likely to work. The point here isn't whether or not to hit; it's that the advice you read may directly contradict your own (admittedly powerful) experience. Clarifying explanations would be helpful, but they aren't always there, or aren't always clear. (The reason, by the way, that I personally don't recommend hitting back is that in the current climate, this strategy is likely to backfire. The first thing a bully may do is go tell an authority figure that he's been hit, and now the original target will be the one in trouble. Not only that, the bully can easily take revenge online.)

Faced with all this – the contradictions, the inapplicability of your own experiences, and the lack of traditional parenting support (read: your own parents) – you could easily end up fruitlessly debating the situation in your own mind. Your own experiences matter, but maybe they were more relevant in a bygone world; one expert says one thing, another has entirely different advice. Maybe if your child hits back, it'll just worsen the entire situation. On the other hand, if he succeeds, perhaps the experience will increase his self-confidence immensely. This back-and-forth is all well and good in academic circles; but in real life, faced with a crisis, it can add to the frustration instead of helping resolve the problem.

Bullying and cyberbullying certainly aren't the only areas of parenting that feature a great deal of competing advice, but it's a notable challenge because the problems are often totally unexpected and can feel incomprehensible. Other areas of parenting that invite differing opinions may not be so complex or changeable. Should you make children eat vegetables? Allow them to sleep in your bed? Send them to a private school? Make them clean up the kitchen? Even the most widely agreed-upon issues are sometimes debated. Most people encourage kids to share, but a mom once asked me, "Why should I make my kids share? Grownups never have to share anything."[4] You may or may not have the answers for all the typical dilemmas like these, but at least you understand the questions. In the case of bullying, though, the quagmire of information makes it unclear what we're actually talking about. What is social cruelty? It can be a problem that will simply pass – but we're also told it can be permanently scarring. A 2015 review of the long-term studies on bullying concluded that bullying had negative effects on a target's emotions, cognitions, and relationships.[5] And what is the right response? Intervening can be destructive in some situations but helpful in others. How can you tease apart the serious situations where *not* intervening could lead to serious depression or problems, versus a transient episode where your child (or you!) could learn to stand up and be assertive? If you do intervene, you might be crippling an emerging ability to defend oneself; but if you don't intervene, you might be risking emotional, social, and even academic problems.

The myths that surround bullying and cyberbullying foster all these dilemmas and frustrations, and they're what I'm going to tackle here. I could talk about 25 facts; but instead, I'm going to discuss 25 pieces of misinformation that are common but that also might be hampering your ability to clearly understand and effectively cope with these problems. Generally speaking, these aren't what I would call *senseless* myths, like believing that bullies are possessed by demons. Our modern-day myths about bullying and cyberbullying often were once helpful pieces of information; put simply, bullying and cyberbullying have changed so much in the last 15 years that it's hard for the advice to keep pace. But it's important to have accurate information. As adults, we won't be able to prevent or intervene in bullying and cyberbullying if we can't accurately identify and respond to it. If you don't know, for example, what types of psychological bullying or cyberbullying are the most common types, you won't know what to look for, you might not recognize it when it happens, and you won't be able to help your child form coping strategies.

But just the facts (or just the myths) aren't enough, for a few reasons. First, in real life, while there are always notable exceptions to the rule, sometimes we confuse the exception and the rule. It's hard to know what's common and what's rare. As an example, take the fact that most bullying today is psychological, not physical. This trend is undeniable – even by 2012, 88% of the incidents I studied in my research were psychological in nature. But that doesn't mean *every single case* is only psychological. If you vividly recall being physically bullied as a child, the intensity of that memory makes it hard to accept the idea that bullying today isn't, for the most part, physical. When your own child is being shoved into his locker at school every day, it's hard to believe that his experience is actually much less common, and even harder to see why such trends matter. (Indeed, in that case, they might not.) The facts about bullying and cyberbullying aren't absolute – they are guidelines, but important ones, since they help us know what to look for and how to react when we find it. If you read somewhere that "torn clothing" is a good indication of bullying, you're going to fail to notice an awful lot (since verbal bullying and cyberbullying obviously don't tear anyone's clothes). No one type of bullying accounts for 100% of the cases, but the best way to identify bullying is still to learn to recognize where and how it's most likely to be manifested. Ultimately, parents need to know the facts, the frequent variations, and the personal and emotional experiences that can surround these issues.

The second reason it's not enough to simply list facts about bullying and cyberbullying is that such an approach ignores the reality that these behaviors are sometimes associated with other, much more devastating, outcomes (such as severe emotional damage and even death). Does bullying cause depression and possibly suicide? Does it cause homicidal behavior? When a particular incident (usually in the news media) seems to highlight a possible association between bullying and a catastrophic outcome, it can be difficult to shake the feeling that bullying is terribly dangerous, even if you have the facts at your fingertips. Bullying may not often contribute to suicide, but if you have a depressed, bullied child, that may be a risk you're not willing to ignore. (Nor should you.) When the stakes are high, we're motivated to pay attention even to small probabilities. Consider: overall, it's not likely that you'll die in a car crash; but even so, no one denies the value and importance of safety belts.

Understand the myths, because myths can ultimately impede your ability to cope and your ability to help your child learn to cope. Thinking that a catastrophic outcome (like suicide) is common – when it's not – can invoke paralyzing anxiety and fear. You're so scared of suicide that you might ignore the bullying. Lack of knowledge can mean using the wrong tactics, or none at all. Maybe you encourage your child to hit back, and she is subsequently suspended from school. Not knowing what to look for can cause either over-attribution (characterizing something that's not bullying as bullying) or under-attribution (failing to see bullying or cyberbullying when it happens).

So in this book, instead of staking out absolute "factual" positions (i.e. *it is true* or *it isn't true*), I'm going to take a look at both the most recent trends in bullying and cyberbullying research *and* the complexity that defines 25 of the most common myths. Dealing with bullying and cyberbullying is all about prevention and strategy; and because, frankly, it's not always a 100% fixable problem, it's also about increasing coping skills, social support, and resiliency. The questions we ask our children and the assumptions we make have a big impact on the tactics we discuss with our kids and the success they ultimately have.

My own vantage point is somewhat unique. I'm a researcher and a professor, and my 30 years of research and teaching focus on bullying, aggression, *and* digital technology (a somewhat odd, but actually quite useful, combination). I'm also a parent who's had to deal with my own children's experiences of social cruelty, as well as deal with all the chaos, tension, and difficulty surrounding the use of digital technology in any home with modern kids. My experience as a mother has taught me how challenging and frustrating this issue can be and how much we can long for fast, easy, ripping-off-the-Band-Aid solutions. I know how hard it is to see my kids feeling hurt, and how tempting it is to try to fix everything for them. But it's my longstanding professional interest as a researcher and a teacher, and my relationships with colleagues both in North America and in Europe, that have most strongly guided my perspective. When considering how to help children with these problems, I think it's critical to take into account how kids develop and how digital technology really impacts human communication and human relationships. It's the juxtaposition of these two areas of knowledge that I'll bring to this book. If your expectation is an instant resolution, you should know up front that this problem can defy quick solutions. *But there is relief to be had.* Not perfection – but relief.

You may find yourself wanting to hold unto some of the myths I describe here. It's important to remember that myths about bullying and cyberbullying aren't fantasies, make-believe, silly, or baseless. It's easy to dismiss myths that have no history of real evidence: you probably know that the Earth isn't flat and that crossing your eyes doesn't make them stick that way. It's a lot more difficult to dismiss beliefs or strategies that were once essentially correct, but that aren't today. As the world shifts and changes, explanations that were spot-on a generation ago can indeed become completely wrong – sometimes dismayingly so. Fifty years ago, an American with only a high school diploma could land a job that would enable him or her to maintain a middle-class lifestyle. But today, it would be a myth to say that a high school education is all you need to live in the middle class. The rapidity of these types of social changes is why myths about bullying and cyberbullying can be among the toughest to challenge. Let's get started.

Notes

1. DiIulio Jr., J.J. (1995). Moral poverty: The coming of the super-predators should scare us into wanting to get to the root causes of crime a lot faster. *Chicago Tribune* (15 December), p. 31.

2. C.S. Mott Children's Hospital. (2017). Mott Poll report: Bullying and internet safety are top health concerns for parents. https://mottpoll.org/reports-surveys/bullying-and-internet-safety-are-top-health-concerns-parents.

3. Bully Police USA. (2017). www.bullypolice.org.

4. I wasn't able to resist pointing out to her that adults share many, many things – a home, money, bathrooms, childrearing decisions, daily chores, etc.

5. Wolke, D. and Lereya, S.T. (2015). Long-term effects of bullying. *Archives of Disease in Childhood* 100 (9): 879–885. https://doi.org/10.1136/archdischild-2014-306667.

Chapter 2
Myth #1
Bullying is usually about a big kid beating up a smaller kid.

The deadliest animal in the world isn't the crocodile or the bear – it's actually the mosquito.[1] This persistent, tiny pest kills much more effectively and efficiently than any enraged bear by simply carrying malaria, yellow fever, and other blood-borne illnesses. But while we're not likely to hear a tabloid news story about an outbreak of malaria, a bear attack on a few hikers is much more dramatic and makes much better news copy (even if it is statistically far less lethal). In 2016, many news outlets carried the sad story of a well-liked Forest Service officer who was suddenly killed by a bear in Montana; in the same year, thousands of people died from malaria in Tanzania alone.[2]

25 Myths About Bullying and Cyberbullying, First Edition.
Elizabeth K. Englander.
© 2020 John Wiley & Sons, Inc. Published 2020 by John Wiley & Sons, Inc.

In a similar way, severe incidents of physical attacks and bullying might be the most salient and noticeable, but it's that persistent and contemporary pest – psychological bullying – that really affects most of us. Yet until relatively recently, most researchers and educators focused on the type of bullying that was most evident and easiest to detect: physical harassment that happened on school grounds. Even as recently as 2015, the very first item on the National Education Association's list of "signs of bullying" was "torn clothes," despite overwhelming data that psychological injuries prevail.[3]

The fact is that physical bullying is in many ways easier to address, because it simplifies and clarifies the role adults should play and how they can respond. Although it's not always a simple task to spot a bullying situation when the bullying is psychological, detecting physical bullying isn't as hard – there are obvious, concrete signs. The relatively less complex nature of physical bullying makes it a tempting area for our focus, and the more difficult job of assessing psychological damage tempts us to brush it aside.

It's important, though, to keep your eye on the ball. A slew of research has overwhelmingly concluded that most bullying happening in the third decade of the twenty-first century is, indeed, *psychological* in nature – either verbal or relational, in person, or through digital technology.[4] In one of my own research studies, where I've examined thousands of 18-year-olds at the university where I've taught for many years, I've found exactly that same pattern. I've also studied more than 50,000 children aged 8–18, and those findings agree; far more children report being psychologically victimized by bullies, compared to the number who report that they're being physically targeted. Just as psychological bullying appears to be gaining in popularity, physical bullying seems to be declining precipitously.[5] It hasn't completely disappeared, but it's most definitely taken a back seat to its sneakier, less apparent but arguably more damaging cousin.[6] These findings are far from isolated. Other researchers have noted the same trend.[7,8,9]

The fact that most bullying today is psychological probably represents a major social shift, the result of profound changes in how we raise children, our tolerance of aggression, and the role of digital technology. Back when physical bullying was the focus, a child's size had real implications for becoming a bully. A 1998 study of three-year-olds found that preschoolers who were at least half an inch taller than their peers were actually more likely to be physically aggressive at age 11.[10] Attacking or threatening your target with physical violence carried with it certain implications – the primary one being that when you used physical bullying, you had to carry out your bullying away from adult eyes. Avoiding adults is less of a problem for today's bullies. This is ironic, considering that children today are more closely supervised, spend less time away from adults, and generally find that adults tolerate aggression less than they once did. I think that most modern parents (myself included) approve of supervision and less aggression. But these positive social changes have also incurred a cost. While more supervision and less tolerance for aggression have hampered physical bullying, they may have also motivated bullies to perfect psychological tactics in the social power dance. "Game of Thrones" – the school edition – persists, and psychological attacks are, unfortunately, much more advantageous. For one thing, they can be carried out right in front of adults through the use of subtle behaviors and through digital technology, which, despite its myriad rewards, has (it must be admitted) helped facilitate this type of problem.[11]

Just because psychological tactics predominate, though, doesn't mean they're all the same. The precise behaviors that children use to bully vary notably, depending upon the environment where they occur. In school, kids primarily bully through the use of psychological behaviors that express contempt or dismissiveness – for example, they might ignore a person who's speaking to them, laugh meanly at someone, or roll their eyes when an opinion is voiced or an answer is wrong. In research, we call these *gateway behaviors*, because frequent and widespread expressions of contempt are the "gateway" to more toxic and unpleasant social climates. One form of this is (particularly among girls) *relational aggression*, which is bullying or cruelty in which the aggressor takes action to interfere with friendships or torpedo another's relationships as a way of hurting the target.[12] In digital realms (online in gaming and social media, or through exchanging digital messages such as text messaging), psychological bullying might feature biting comments, threats, or public humiliation. Digital bullying can be relational and/or contemptuous. Both in school *and* online, though, the single most common type of meanness and bullying is often both relational *and* contemptuous: spreading gossip and rumors, which may or may not be true and which can enormously impact friendships. (In virtually every school where my students and colleagues at the Massachusetts Aggression Reduction Center work, rumors and gossip play a key, prominent role in making life difficult for the students [by their own admission].) The primary challenge in reducing gossip and rumors is (not to put too fine a point on it) its self-reinforcing nature. The fact is, it's *fun* to gossip. And that makes it hard to resist, and hard to suppress.

All of these things – gateway behaviors, relational aggression, and digital meanness – are relatively common in childhood and adolescence. But please note (and this is important!):

I'm not saying that every rumor, or every contemptuous behavior, necessarily constitutes bullying.

More often than not, gateway behaviors are used just to be mean (perhaps without really thinking), to show off, or when two kids are fighting and mad at each other. In other words, bullying is only *one* reason kids would use these behaviors. Characterizing every eye roll as bullying would be crazy; but it's not crazy to say that eye-rolling is one way of making a victim of bullying feel terrible, and a way of continuing the saga of cruelty against them. When gateway behaviors are used sporadically or in isolation, the hurt is likewise transient. But if they're used as part and parcel of an ongoing campaign to make someone's life miserable, the impact is often much more potent.

One challenge that's interesting to me is how two-faced we are as a society about gateway behaviors and relational aggression. On the one hand, generally speaking, our social rules dictate that we shouldn't use behaviors that openly express contempt for others.

We're taught not to whisper to someone in front of other people, not to make a face when introduced to someone, and not to call others mean names (at least, not to their face). In practice, though, we sometimes tolerate these snarky behaviors – particularly, but not exclusively, when they're used by children. So although we might hasten to correct a child who says aloud, "You're an idiot," we may do nothing when that same child rolls his eyes, even though that gesture is essentially a nonverbal way of implying the same thing. Although I know of no data supporting this point, I think an argument could be made that we've become more tolerant of these rude behaviors in children – more inclined, perhaps, to excuse rudeness by attributed it to "adolescence" or "just being a kid," and less likely to correct it. Perhaps we sometimes view such social rules as superficial, arbitrary, or pointless; why shouldn't we tell people they're stupid if we think they are? Yet when we dispense with the guidelines that demand social civility, the result can be a psychological climate that is decidedly unpleasant and even hurtful. I think that behaving politely even when you don't admire someone is an important social mechanism that has evolved to keep our society agreeable. It makes everyone feel more relaxed and content – not just the target of that (so-called) "fake" politeness. In contrast, behaving contemptuously toward those you don't admire makes all onlookers feel uncomfortable – again, not just the target. If the incivility is actually celebrated as courage or honesty, others may decide to take up gateway behaviors and relational aggression. The fact that these behaviors affect *everyone* in the environment (not just targets) is an essential fact that we all need to remember. You may have heard that bullying prevention is all about "improving the climate." This is what that means.

But social problems aren't just about whether or not a behavior hurts; they are also about *how much* it hurts. It would be reasonable to assume that psychological attacks don't hurt as much as physical attacks. We all recall the "sticks and stones can break my bones, but words will never hurt me" saying. But in reality, the data suggest that the opposite is true. (Maybe the saying is wishful thinking.) One way to study this is to assess how hurtful cyberbullying is (since cyberbullying is exclusively psychological). In the 2013–2014 school year, I studied this issue in a sample of 421 teenagers. Among many other questions, I asked them about being targeted by their peers online, in school, in both places, or in neither place. The students who were targeted online (or both online and in school) reported being much more emotionally impacted, compared to the students who were attacked in person. This might seem ridiculous – how could words on a screen be so hurtful? (I once wrote a paper entitled *Just Turn the Darn Thing Off.*[13]) That question is really part of a larger question: how can psychological attacks hurt more than physical attacks?

But in reality, there are good reasons why psychological attacks can hurt more. First, psychological attacks can be much more sustained than physical attacks; they can go on and on, and they often cross over from school to cyberspace to continue even further.[14] Second, because they can often be done right in front of others using digital means, gateway behaviors, or relational aggression, they can be much more public. That public exposure can be a key element in the trauma induced by bullying and cyberbullying, and it is, unfortunately, often exacerbated by adolescent psychology. During the teenage years, boys and girls have a distinct feeling that the entire world is watching them and endlessly fascinated by them. Psychologists term this effect an *imaginary audience* – the sense that you're constantly on stage, being closely examined by everyone else. This helps explain why your teenager might refuse to go to school because of a tiny pimple on their face. Adults might realize that a minor flaw isn't terribly noticeable, but for an adolescent who feels like they're under constant intense scrutiny, even a small flaw is assumed to be quite noticeable indeed. All this makes it very hard for teens to shrug off any public incidents.

This cognitive tendency, coupled with the dynamics of digital interactions, can actually worsen the impact of a teen's negative exposure. Online, a much broader circle of peers can participate in discussions or conversations (in real time or delayed). That can be, and usually is, very appealing. But the downside is that everything negative is also very public. In one of my studies, I asked teens how long it would take for a digital rumor to get around a school to 100 kids; most answered that it would take 15 minutes or less. If a friend gets mad at you and tries to humiliate you at the mall, odds are that at most there will be only a few witnesses. But online, the number of witnesses feels endless – and thus the attack feels potentially much more humiliating. So even though cyberbullying can only be psychological, it can also be very distressing. That sense that everyone's aware of your humiliation is key to understanding why psychological bullying can be so traumatic.

Realistically, we can't completely change the adolescent tendency to over-focus on oneself. But we can keep in mind how much psychological attacks can hurt, particularly in the teenage years, and we can remind our kids that most other teens are more interested in themselves than in others. It's ironic that adolescents can feel so humiliated by a rumor or negative event and so sure that everyone is focused on their humiliation, when the fact is that most teens are focused simply on how they themselves are appearing to others. Sometimes taking the long view can help kids cope with the trauma at hand.

To-Do for Myth #1: Bullying is usually about a big kid beating up a smaller kid.

The reality: Most bullying is psychological.

Although parents shouldn't exist in a constant state of paranoia about bullying and cyberbullying, it's a good idea to pay attention to how your children are doing socially, and how they're feeling about their friends and peers. Never assume that because you don't see obvious signs – like bruises – everything must be all right. The difficulty is how

(continued)

(*continued*)

to talk about these issues with your kids. Here are a few ideas of easy ways to start those conversations:

1. Take advantage of stories you hear on the news or in your community. If there's a story about a bad situation or another child who's a victim, use that story to ask your child about his or her own experiences. Do they think the news story is exaggerated? Is it accurate? Do they see or know about or experience bullying, and what does it look like?

2. Ask your child what kinds of programs their school offers, and ask them their serious opinion of these programs. Are they silly? Boring? Do they miss the point? Were good ideas spread around, or new concepts that they hadn't considered before?

3. Tell your child that you're aware there's a lot of adult anxiety around the idea of digital devices and how kids use them. Ask their opinion about this anxiety, and ask if kids sometimes feel anxious too. What apps or programs are their favorites, and what's fun about them? If they had advice for their younger siblings, or younger kids in general, what would they say, and what do they think younger kids should be taught?

Note: the goal of these conversations can't be to get the skinny the first time out of the box. Your goals are actually fairly simple: you want your child to know that you're interested in these problems and, furthermore, that you're interested in *their opinions and thoughts*. Don't worry if you're brushed off at first. Ask their opinion, and ask it genuinely; that's a tactic few targets of conversation are able to entirely resist.

Notes

1. Ronca, D. (2008). Which animals kill the most people in the wild? HowStuffWorks.com. http://adventure.howstuffworks.com/dangerous-animals1.htm (accessed 11 July 2014).

2. World Health Organization. (2014). Atlas of African Health Statistics. https://www.humanitarianresponse.info/sites/www.humanitarianresponse.info/files/documents/files/AFRO-Statistical_Factsheet.pdf.

3. National Education Association. Parents' role in bullying and intervention. http://www.nea.org/home/56805.htm (accessed 11 July 2014).

4. Kowalski, R.M., Giumetti, G.W., Schroeder, A.N. et al. (2014). Bullying in the digital age: a critical review and meta-analysis of cyberbullying research among youth. *Psychological Bulletin* 140 (4): 1073–1137. https://doi.org/10.1037/a0035618.

5. Finkelhor, D., Turner, H., Ormrod, R. et al. (2010). Trends in childhood violence and abuse exposure: evidence from 2 national surveys. *Archives of Pediatrics & Adolescent Medicine* 164 (3): 238–242. https://doi.org/10.1001/archpediatrics.2009.283.

6. Englander, E. (2013). *Bullying and Cyberbullying: What Every Educator Needs to Know.* Cambridge, Mass: Harvard Education Press.

7. Coulter, R., Kessel, S., Schneider, S. et al. (2012). Cyberbullying, school bullying, and psychological distress: a regional census of high school students. *American Journal of Public Health* 102 (1): 171–177, http://ajph.aphapublications.org/cgi/content/abstract/AJPH.2011.300308v1.

8. Ando, M. (2005). Psychosocial influences on physical, verbal, and indirect bullying among Japanese early adolescents. *The Journal of Early Adolescence* 25 (3): 268–297. https://doi.org/10.1177/0272431605276933.

9. Coyne, S.M., Linder, J., Nelson, D. et al. (2012). "Frenemies, Fraitors, and Mean-Em-Aitors": priming effects of viewing physical and relational aggression in the media on women. *Aggressive Behavior* 38 (2): 141–149. https://doi.org/10.1002/ab.21410.

10. Raine, A., Reynolds, C., Venables, P. et al. (1998). Fearlessness, stimulation-seeking, and large body size at age 3 years as early predispositions to childhood aggression at age 11 years. *Archives of General Psychiatry* 55 (8): 745. https://doi.org/10.1001/archpsyc.55.8.745.

11. Perhaps this is a good time to insert a caveat, namely, that I am not against digital technology or its use; that I believe that the Internet has greatly enhanced modern life in many ways, although it has cost us too; and that

our children, who will always be heavy technology users, need to learn and practice how to use digital technology, which includes when and how *not* to use it.

12. Wang, J., Iannotti, R., and Nansel, T. (2009). School bullying among adolescents in the United States: physical, verbal, relational, and cyber. *Journal of Adolescent Health* 45 (4): 368–375. https://doi.org/10.1016/j.jadohealth.2009.03.021.

13. Englander, E. and Muldowney, A. (2007). Just turn the darn thing off: understanding cyberbullying. In: *Proceedings of Persistently Safe Schools: The 2007 National Conference on Safe Schools* (ed. D.L. White, B.C. Glenn, and A. Wimes), 83–92. Washington, DC: Hamilton Fish Institute, The George Washington University.

14. Schneider, S.K., O'Donnell, L., Stueve, A., and Coulter, R.W.S. (2012). Cyberbullying, school bullying, and psychological distress: a regional census of high school students. *Am J Public Health* 102 (1): 171–177.

Chapter 3
Myth #2
Bullying causes suicide and homicide.

** WARNING **

Many parents are understandably worried about the idea that bullying could lead to violence or suicide. And because this is a complicated issue, I'm going to take the time and the space to explain it in detail.

Let's start with what we know and how we know it.

Obviously, some diseases have a clear and simple cause. In those cases, we know that A causes B. The rubeola virus is present in every person who has the measles, so we know that the rubeola virus causes measles. But when it comes to human behavior, that type of clear, simple relationship is unusual. In psychology, most of the time we speak of factors that *contribute* to behavior or make it more likely, instead of outright causing it.

25 Myths About Bullying and Cyberbullying, First Edition.
Elizabeth K. Englander.
© 2020 John Wiley & Sons, Inc. Published 2020 by John Wiley & Sons, Inc.

The mass media, though, prefers simple relationships. A headline reading "BULLYING CONTRIBUTES TO SUICIDE ... MAYBE" just doesn't pack the punch of "BULLYING VICTIM DRIVEN TO SUICIDE!" In a nutshell, there is scientific evidence regarding *how* bullying and cyberbullying are related to homicide or suicide; but the mass media's reporting often seems to inflate our perception of the simplicity, strength, and consistency of that relationship. Dr. Jorge Srabstein conducted a very interesting study of how bullying, injury, and death are handled in modern media.[1] He combed through news reports published throughout North and South America and found that the news media's portrayal of bullying skewed markedly toward the most severe cases. The truth is that only a very tiny fraction of real bullying cases are related to a fatality, but fully 43% of the cases that appeared in the news involved a fatality. Of these, about half involved suicides and half involved homicides. The media's relentless focus on more serious aggression and outcomes is unlikely to be a deliberate attempt to mislead people, but it still has the effect of leaving the public with a lopsided impression of the risks associated with bullying and cyberbullying.

One of the first blockbuster media stories that linked being a victim of bullying to homicide was the school shooting at Columbine High School in Littleton, Colorado in 1999. In the wake of that shooting, the United States Secret Service conducted a study of school shootings that happened in the 1990s. That study concluded that bullying was a common, although not universal, factor in the background of school shooters: 71% of these homicidal kids felt that they had been victims of bullying or harassment.[2] These statistics stoke the fear that bullying could turn normal children into cold-blooded killers. The Secret Service study did look to see if the school shooters appeared to be relatively normal; however, the study didn't probe for psychopathology, instead only checking for the most general indicators of functioning, like the shooters' grades. The study didn't detect any rampant signs of mental illness or significantly compromised functioning in these violent students. Most kids who became shooters were passing their classes, and some were even excelling academically. Socially, though, a few more problems emerged. More than half of the shooters showed signs of social problems, either being part of a disliked group of students, being "loners," or experiencing social rejection. But even social problems weren't universal. Many school shooters had social problems, and many were probably bullied. But not all.

That study and others suggested the theory that bullying and social problems might be one factor that increased the likelihood of homicidal behavior. Bullying was more common among school shooters, but it wasn't always present in the histories of school shooters. By the way, this is a perfect example of why we can't precisely predict violence in human beings. Although we do know that some risk factors (like social problems and bullying) increase the odds that someone will be violent, not all violent people have histories of social problems or being bullied; and many individuals are bullied or have social problems but never become violent at all. Bullying is a risk factor, not a direct cause.[3] What we don't understand as well is *why* bullying may be associated with violence in some cases, while it isn't in so many. It's unsettling, but the fact remains that there is no exact recipe.

The risk of suicide among victims of bullying has received much more attention. Depending on what you've seen or read, you might come away with different impressions of this problem. The terrible suicides of Carl Walker-Hoover and Phoebe Prince, 11- and 16-year-old victims of bullying from Massachusetts, provoked a firestorm of coverage in the media in 2009 and 2010. That media tsunami that followed their deaths featured a great deal of discussion about a possible link between suicide, bullying, and cyberbullying. Reading those and other news stories about teenagers who have committed suicide could lead anyone to conclude that suicide is not only associated with bullying, but *strongly* associated with it, and a perfectly happy child could abruptly decide to commit suicide after being bullied or cyberbullied possibly even just briefly. More authoritative voices have also underlined the possibility of this relationship. *Medical News Today* describes the link between bullying and suicide-related behaviors as "close,"[4] and a study in the United Kingdom reported that more than one-third of bullied teens were suicidal.[5]

But take a step back, and you'll see that the knowledge just isn't so definitive. While some stories suggest a strong link, researchers have consistently found a more tempered and nuanced relationship between bullying, cyberbullying, and suicide. Bullying and cyberbullying do appear to have a relationship to suicide, but the nature of that relationship may be indirect and influenced by other factors. For example, it's hard to tease apart the role of bullying versus depression and other emotional problems in leading to suicide. Can bullying or cyberbullying lead to suicide even in the absence of other problems like depression? We may assume that the formula is "bullying → depression → suicide," but there must be many cases where this deceptively simple formula doesn't really work. For example, can bullying ultimately can lead to suicide even in a child who is very healthy, emotionally and socially? What if a child is already depressed and possibly suicidal before they're bullied? Could the bullying be experienced as just another problem, or even as something insignificant compared to their preexisting depression and/or suicidality? Why do some depressed and bullied kids commit suicide while others don't?

A review in 2010 of the existing research found that most studies linking suicide and bullying either didn't take depression or psychopathology into account or, if they did, found that these emotional difficulties accounted for the relationship between bullying and suicidality.[6] In other words, these studies found that depression was a more powerful influence in leading to suicide than bullying per se. Having said that, most of the research in this area is conducted by measuring suicidality and bullying at the same point in time, which tells us these factors are related but doesn't give us much information about what causes what. This might seem silly – it can seem obvious that bullying can cause depression, which in turn can cause suicidality. But I can imagine a scenario in which, for example, depression causes a child to consider suicide and also causes them to bully others and to be bullied themselves. In that kind of case, depression would be the root cause of both bullying involvement and suicidality. I can also imagine a scenario where bullying combines with other stressors to cause both depression and suicidality.

Having complicated all this for you, there are some things we do know with some certainty. We know that depression can lead to suicide. And it's not hard to see how a combination of multiple stressors can increase the odds of suicide. Phoebe Prince was depressed and cutting herself before her peers piled on the bullying.[7] What's much less clear, though, is whether bullying by itself could lead to suicide in a child who's not depressed. Perhaps bullying can be unrelated to depression at the time of the bullying but leave the person more vulnerable to depression later in life. The pathway from bullying to suicide might even be different for different genders. A Finnish study found that being bullied frequently (not once) increased suicidality later in life for girls, regardless of the presence or absence of depression; but in boys, just being a victim wasn't related to later suicidality unless the boy was *also* a bully (often termed a *bully/victim*), and had a conduct disorder, in which case there was a significantly increased risk of later suicidality.[8]

How does all this help in any practical sense? We can say with some confidence that bullying may sometimes increase the risk of suicidal thoughts or actions, particularly in girls and particularly when other problems, such as depression, bullying others, or conduct disorders, are also present. Equally important, though, bullying and cyberbullying do not simply cause suicidality in everyone, or even in most people. Boys and girls seem to have different pathways of vulnerability. But how does that translate into risk for a parent who knows their child is being bullied (or is bullying) and is worried about the possibility of suicide? There are two big questions that I tend to hear in these circumstances.

3.1 Question #1: Can being bullied cause a child to begin thinking about suicide?

Thinking about suicide is called *suicidal ideation*, and suicidal ideation doesn't always lead to actual suicide; but it is a very important and serious risk factor. Any child who thinks about suicide – whether or not they've been bullied or bully others – should be immediately taken to see a healthcare professional. A number of studies have found that, particularly but not only in girls, being bullied can increase the chance of suicidal ideation even among those who are not depressed.[9] So the answer is a qualified yes: being bullied is *sometimes* associated with suicidal ideation; but it's important to remember that *thinking* about suicide and *attempting* suicide are two different things. Thinking about suicide is an urgent symptom that calls for a professional assessment. Attempting to commit suicide is a medical emergency – which leads to our second question.

3.2 Question #2: When should a parent be most worried about bullying leading to suicidal thoughts or actions?

It's clear that we don't know all the risk factors, but we can pay attention to the ones we do know about. The research suggests that the risk is greatest when the child is already struggling, or begins struggling, with additional emotional difficulties, behavior problems, or any other types of trauma. So a child who has had evidence of conduct disorders, depression, or past suicidality should be assessed if they are also being bullied. They should also be seen if they are struggling with other types of traumas or stressors, such as substance abuse, the death or serious illness of someone significant to them, family changes such as divorce, child abuse, expulsion from school, etc. Some kids are more vulnerable than others: for example, LGBTQ children may be chronic victims of social exclusion and thus might need more attention and care. The bottom line is that parents need to be aware of the signs of depression and look for these in their child. They may want to look especially carefully if they are aware that their child is being bullied or may be particularly vulnerable.

These two questions are the ones I hear the most, but they are not the only questions that remain. For example, perhaps being bullied at one age versus another is more closely linked to suicidality. At this time, researchers usually don't compare different age groups, so no real consensus has emerged, although the risk of suicide in general increases as children begin to go through adolescence.[10] Another pertinent question often arises regarding the psychological impact of cyberbullying. A few studies have found that cyberbullying may be more strongly related to suicidal ideation, relative to traditional bullying[11,12] (although, as you'll read in future chapters, separating the two types of bullying today doesn't make much sense). Finally, how can we tell when children and teens are actually depressed? The best method is to regularly see, talk to, and spend time with your child, so you are more apt to notice changes in their mood or behavior. Having said that, there is no absolute, completely reliable indicator – unfortunately. When you're unsure, consult a professional. It's fine to start with your pediatrician or family doctor.

To-Do for Myth #2: Bullying causes suicide and homicide.
The truth: This relationship is neither simple nor direct.

What if your child isn't the type to talk with you about their social problems or their feelings? You can't force someone to disclose private thoughts to you, and punishing them for not talking will only push them further away. On the other hand, modeling what you're looking for – conversations about social relationships and feelings – can show your child that you're interested in their social lives and how they're feeling. So, take opportunities that come along to begin conversations. When a friend walks by, you could say to your child, "It was nice to see Henry again; are you two still as good friends as you used to be?" Don't be too concerned if all you get is a shrug or a grunt. These kinds of

(continued)

(*continued*)

conversations are designed for the long haul; your goal is not just to get information – it's to show genuine interest and to encourage your child to talk when things get tough, because that is a key strategy that helps all of us to cope. After a while, you may begin to hear some real answers to your questions.

Talking to your child – and encouraging them to talk to you – pays off both in terms of the effort and in terms of your ability to detect serious problems when they arise. Many children (especially teenagers) are not inclined to talk with their parents about these issues, but many do ultimately respond when they're gently encouraged to do so. Don't forget, either, that you're not in this alone. Kids can also be encouraged to speak with others, such as their pediatrician, teachers, adult relatives, etc.

When you *are* talking, listen for changes or indications of depression or hopelessness. If anything alarms or worries you, consult with your pediatrician or family doctor about an assessment and getting help.

Notes

1. Srabstein, J.C. (2013). News reports of bullying-related fatal and nonfatal injuries in the Americas. *Revista Panamericana De Salud Pública = Pan American Journal of Public Health* 33 (5): 378–382.
2. Fein, R., Reddy, M., Borum, R. et al. (2002). *The Final Report and Findings of the Safe School Initiative : Implications for the Prevention of School Attacks in the United States*. Washington, DC: U.S. Secret Service. https://www2.ed.gov/admins/lead/safety/preventingattacksreport.pdf.
3. A *risk factor* is something that increases the risk of disease without necessarily being a direct cause. For example, not wearing a seat belt is a risk factor for being killed in a car crash. The seat belt doesn't cause the crash,

but not wearing it is statistically associated with a worse outcome if a crash does happen.

4. Nordqvist, C. (2013). Strong link between bullying and suicide. *Medical News Today* (June 19). http://www.medicalnewstoday.com/articles/262150.php.

5. Ditch the Label. (2018). Annual bullying survey. https://www.ditchthelabel.org/research-papers/the-annual-bullying-survey-2018 (accessed November 22, 2019).

6. Klomek, A.B., Sourander, A., and Gould, M. (2010). The association of suicide and bullying in childhood to young adulthood: a review of cross-sectional and longitudinal research findings. *Canadian Journal of Psychiatry. Revue Canadienne De Psychiatrie* 55 (5): 282–288.

7. Bazelon, E. (2010). The untold story of her suicide and the role of the kids who have been criminally charged for it. *Slate Magazine* (July 21). https://slate.com/human-interest/2010/07/what-really-happened-to-phoebe-prince-the-untold-story-of-her-suicide-and-the-role-of-the-kids-who-have-been-criminally-charged-for-it-1.html.

8. Klomek, A.B., Sourander, A., Niemela, S. et al. (2009). Childhood bullying behaviors as a risk for suicide attempts and completed suicides: a population-based birth cohort study. *Journal of the American Academy of Child & Adolescent Psychiatry* 48 (3): 254–261. https://doi.org/10.1097/CHI.0b013e318196b91f.

9. Kaminski, J.W. and Fang, X. (2009). Victimization by peers and adolescent suicide in three US samples. *The Journal of Pediatrics* 155 (5): 683–688. https://doi.org/10.1016/j.jpeds.2009.04.061.

10. Klomek, A.B., Sourander, A., and Gould, M. (2010). The association of suicide and bullying in childhood to young adulthood: a review of cross-sectional and longitudinal research findings. *Canadian Journal of Psychiatry. Revue Canadienne De Psychiatrie* 55 (5): 282–288.

11. van Geel, M., Vedder, P., and Tanilon, J. (2014). Relationship between peer victimization, cyberbullying, and suicide in children and adolescents: a meta-analysis. *JAMA Pediatrics* 168 (5): 435–442. https://doi.org/10.1001/jamapediatrics.2013.4143.

12. Hinduja, S. and Patchin, J.W. (2010). Bullying, cyberbullying, and suicide. *Archives of Suicide Research* 14 (3): 206–221. https://doi.org/10.1080/13811118.2010.494133.

Chapter 4
Myth #3
Bullying is a normal part of childhood.

"I got these subtle clues that my girlfriend was seeing someone else. So one day, I trailed her from her office, and you know what? She was taking night classes to get a better job. I felt like such a loser."[1]

In milder forms, a lot of behaviors and feelings can be normal and even productive; but if they're taken too far, the same behaviors and feelings can also cause serious relationship problems. Jealousy is a good example. Everyone has felt jealous at one time or another. It may feel disagreeable, but even normal, psychologically well-adjusted people experience it. Despite being near-universal, it can become pathological in its more extreme forms.[2] Being jealous when your spouse flirts with someone else is normal. Being jealous because they ask a full-service gas station attendant to put 10 gallons of gas

25 Myths About Bullying and Cyberbullying, First Edition.
Elizabeth K. Englander.
© 2020 John Wiley & Sons, Inc. Published 2020 by John Wiley & Sons, Inc.

into their car isn't. Normal jealousy can serve a useful purpose: it may alert someone to potential threats to a relationship. Sometimes that threat can be averted if everyone knows what's going on, and the relationship can thus be saved. Jealousy is no fun to experience, but it probably evolved as a mechanism to help keep couples together.

Unkind behaviors between kids are similar. While peer cruelty during childhood is always unpleasant and often upsetting, it can be either productive or destructive, depending on the circumstances and the intensity of the problems. At low levels, occasional, transient meanness between children can actually be productive. Just as everyone experiences some jealousy, normal social problems also happen almost universally, and severe consequences are generally rare. Some cruelty between children is a developmentally useful part of growing up, by which I mean that while it's no fun to fight with a friend or to hear a malicious remark, the occasional, throwaway nastiness often associated with children's thoughtlessness or impulsivity probably evolved to provide kids with low-risk but challenging social situations that they learn from. How can you learn to handle the much more complicated conflicts of adulthood, if you never learn how to cope with a quarrel during childhood? All children probably need to experience and learn from *a little* mild, random cruelty from peers.

I've seen this principle in action many times, but one incident in particular stands out in my memory. Many years ago, I was briefly observing a group of kindergarteners on a playground. I noticed a little boy who was unhappy because two nearby girls were pointedly whispering and giggling without including him in their joke. Dejectedly, he scanned the playground, spotted another little boy, and trotted over to him. I thought he was going to start playing with the boy, but instead, he dragged him back across the playground and pulled him into a sitting position alongside the two whispering little girls. "Now *we'll* laugh," he happily told the boy; and they did. Not what psychologists would call a prosocial response, exactly; but he was using his exclusion at the hands of these girls to fashion a response that helped him feel more powerful. If the playground monitors had intervened, he might never have learned that social coping skill; and learning that friends are social supports is a critically important technique in dealing with any peer meanness (mild or severe). Indeed, children who are years older report to me in my research that sticking close to their friends is, hands down, the best way to cope with malicious peers.

But what if those girls had excluded that little boy every day? What if this wasn't a one-time event, but part of a persistent series of constant put-downs and expressions of contempt? Like repetitive, serious jealousy, experiencing *repeated, many,* or *severe* social problems dramatically escalates detrimental outcomes. In a study I conducted on more than 400 teens in 2013, I asked subjects how much peer cruelty bothered them. Incidents that met the criteria for true bullying were rated as about 50% more traumatic than fighting, quarrels, or one-time acts of malice. Kids who had a fight with a peer or who had a memorable – but single-incident – act of unkindness done to them rated the experience, on average, at about 51 on a 100-point scale. Bullying victims, though, rated their experiences (on average) at about 73 out of 100 – a significantly higher score. Importantly, it seems to be the *repetitive nature* of bullying that may be the source of damage, rather than whether or not individual acts are severe. For example, social rejection and little cutting remarks may individually seem minor; but, delivered daily, these slights accumulate and can cause real harm. One big but transient embarrassment – for example, enduring a high school rumor about your family – is, in the short term, very upsetting, but research suggests it's less likely to result in the kind of lasting damage that bullying or cyberbullying causes.

Knowing this, the prescription becomes simpler: when the problem isn't too chronic or severe, it's often beneficial for children to learn to cope on their own, albeit (importantly) with coaching, help, and ongoing support from adults and friends. When the problem is part of a pattern of ongoing abuse, though, *even if the individual acts seem minor*, it's no longer a "normal" part of childhood, and adults may need to intervene.

Theoretically, this sounds straightforward, but in practice, I think it's not so simple. Although most adults appreciate the need to ratchet up our responses when real harm does seem likely, determining when something is actually liable to cause such harm is no easy feat. Our desire to tease apart the more from the less serious makes us naturally inclined to search for clues that can indicate the significance of a possible situation, but we sometimes judge situations using unreliable indicators. If a child is crying in front of you, describing an agonizing day at school, do the tears and sobbing mean you're dealing with a crisis like bullying? A friend's daughter felt devastated by an online rumor that she was pregnant (she wasn't) and wept while begging her parents not to make her go to school the next day. Does more upset equal bullying? If a problem seems to be happening over and over again, can it still be "normal" fighting with a friend? If a text message is passed around among hundreds of kids, is that cyberbullying or a rumor that's likely to be passé within two days? These signs are hard to read – not easy, despite their overt nature. While a dramatic emotional reaction is an obvious suggestion that an event is more serious, who would you worry more about: a deeply sad child who says they're being left out a lot, or an upset and agitated child who tells you they're upset because they were cut from the team? As I pointed out earlier, we know it's not necessarily the severity of the event that is most traumatic, but when it's repeated many times. The sad child who's being socially rejected at school over many months may sustain more emotional damage in the end.

The emotions of an upset child aren't the only feelings that can muddy the waters. Other salient, but still possibly misleading, clues are internal; they happen inside of us, but they can be just as prominent as a weeping daughter – and, like that crying face, they can mislead us. Probably the internal triggers I hear about the most are the vivid, emotionally charged memories that all parents have of long-ago insults or moments of humiliation. No one likes these memories, but everyone has them. They're clearly more typical and less extraordinary, and they can make us squirm uncomfortably but usually don't cause the severe kind of trauma that bullying and cyberbullying can lead to.[3] I still have a clear and uncomfortable memory of being laughed at in the seventh grade when a teacher read aloud a note I was passing to my friend during class. These memories do serve a purpose; they're unpleasant, but they probably make us much more sympathetic when our own children undergo social problems. But purposeful or not, they can also cloud our judgment about problems our children undergo. If we've labeled memorably embarrassing or upsetting events as *bullying* (accurately or not), we may generally label similar episodes that our children undergo the same way. For example, if you believe that you were bullied by a date who dumped you right before the school dance, you may find yourself feeling very upset when your child is similarly dumped, and thereby conclude that he's being bullied as well.

So our emotional reaction, or our child's emotional reaction, might not be the best way to decide if a situation is, indeed, bullying. But it's not only that we might pay too much attention to these feelings; there are other important clues that can be mistakenly ignored. I've seen a number of cases where schools and parents engaged in a back-and-forth struggle over a child's social difficulties: *it is bullying – no it isn't bullying*, or something of that nature. This struggle can become so absorbing and intense for the adults that important information about the child's functioning or recovery is completely neglected. Kids have described to me cases where they and their peers have recovered their friendship and/or forgiven one another following an incident, yet their parents – still upset – have continued to aggressively push for the problem to be officially designated as bullying. I've seen cases where a child who is suffering languishes – essentially forgotten – while the adults debate (and sometimes argue) over the label to be applied. The necessary steps to help the child have been completely drowned out by the ensuing duel. This isn't helped when parents don't have faith in the school's response to bullying. One study of parents found that both mothers and fathers often expressed the belief that teachers and administrators were callous, indifferent, or both when it came to handling bullying situations.[4]

Relying on the strength of a child's brief but intense emotional reaction, reacting emotionally because of our own history, or ignoring pertinent information probably results in too many situations being labeled as bullying. I've seen upsetting fights, one-time acts of cruelty, and misinterpretations characterized as bullying or cyberbullying. I remember clearly a mother who described a fight between her daughter and a friend that she mischaracterized as bullying; when I pointed out that it sounded more like a fight, she agreed but added, "Well, it's still bullying to *me*." That emotional tendency to use the word *bullying* to designate anything that's very hurtful is understandable but can cause problems. The fact is that if you define a very common problem (e.g. a quarrel between friends) as *bullying*, then you are in effect making the case that bullying is not extraordinary. If lots of problems are bullying, then many if not most people experience bullying, and thus it becomes, by definition, a normal part of childhood. But if, on the other hand, the word *bullying* is reserved for the much less common repetitive, traumatic, targeted cruelty, then it is clearly *not* a normal part of childhood, and we can hope that people won't treat it as such.

The bottom line is that parents, educators, and kids often have different information about a situation, and they bring with them different emotional experiences; and these can lead to different conclusions. The quest to label incidents as bullying (or not) may cause more problems than it solves. It's important to know if a child is really being bullied, but it's often much more important to understand how the child is coping with a difficult social situation and how adults and friends can help. When there is debate or disagreement about whether a social problem between kids is bullying, parents need to ask themselves a few questions. First, is this determination really necessary in order to help their child adjust? For example, a child who's being excluded because of poor social skills might benefit from a social-skills-building program. A designation of bullying might not have any bearing on their being placed in such a program.

Second, is it possible that other adults are not able to see, or not able to recognize, the problematic behaviors in question? The short answer is yes, but not always. For example, if your child is being ignored socially or called names, those behaviors might not be visible to a teacher or administrator (in the way that a physical attack is obvious). And if an adult does see what's happening, they may conclude that just being ignored isn't particularly serious, without realizing that repetitive social slights can be very damaging indeed. Often I find it's more productive to focus on indications that a child is likely to be truly traumatized and needs our help. Research in this area is uniquely valuable because it can examine hundreds of kids in one fell swoop and assess the impact of different kinds of experiences. The 2013 study I referenced earlier compared children who were more seriously impacted by social traumas with those who were much less affected. In that study, I found that several key factors really seemed to help differentiate between more normal, common peer meanness, and traumatic, chronic events such as bullying and cyberbullying (see this chapter's "To-Do" section for a list of these key factors that can help you differentiate between more- and less-traumatic problems).

Finally, ask yourself this: if the situation *doesn't* seem to be repetitive, intentional, targeted abuse, will designating it as bullying cost your child the opportunity to learn about ways to handle social difficulties? There's a lot a child can learn from having to handle not being invited to a party. Let them consider all the options. Would it be best to let the adults handle things (have your mom call their mom)? Would it help matters to angrily confront the host at school? Maybe it can be helpful emotionally to plan something fun with a friend, to remind yourself that you have people who like you and that this isn't the last party of your lifetime. In the long run, categorizing situations as bullying when they're not might result in your child missing a learning opportunity and maybe being less able to cope socially in the future.

Bullying is an intentional, repetitive, impactful behavior by a more powerful peer. It is not a normal part of childhood, and it is often traumatic. Other social problems can also be traumatic: being targeted by someone you trusted, being publicly humiliated on the Internet, dealing with multiple problems, and having fewer social supports can all be damaging for children. What isn't necessarily as damaging are the types of peer cruelty that *do* seem to be a normal part of childhood: transient quarrels with friends; offhand or careless hurtful remarks; or being cold-shouldered by someone who's mad at you. Bullying and cyberbullying, on the other hand, are neither transient, thoughtless, unintentional, nor typically accompanied swiftly by regret. These actions are more sustained, and thus less ordinary, types of social problems.

To-Do for Myth #3: Bullying is a normal part of childhood.

The truth: Mild, transient, occasional peer meanness is probably part of a normal childhood. Bullying is not.

It can be helpful to know which factors seem to differentiate between more normal types of social problems versus those problems that have a bigger emotional impact:

- Repeated problems result in higher rates of trauma. When a peer does something mean once, especially in front of others, that's hard enough; but when it's happening over and over, you know that you must not only endure this current attack but also look forward to others. That's much tougher for a child to take.
- In my research, kids judged that a problem that migrated online was much more hurtful and impactful than one that happened only in school. In the field, kids often tell me that an attack via digital technology feels more public and thus leaves the target feeling more exposed and vulnerable.
- Interestingly, children who reported feeling attached to a teacher regularly were much less impacted by peer meanness than were students who didn't have that kind of relationship with a teacher.
- Overall, kids who fought a lot with their peers had a harder time coping with peer attacks when they occurred, compared to those who got along better with friends.
- It also appears to be the case that children who are undergoing a social conflict with someone who is, or was recently, a friend report higher levels of distress. (This is completely consistent, by the way, with research

(continued)

on aggression between adults; when the aggressor is a person whom the target feels they should be able to trust – a friend, a spouse, etc. – it's emotionally much more difficult to cope with.)

- Finally, subjects who reported that they were also dealing with other types of stress – parental divorce, sibling illness, family problems, substance abuse, emotional difficulties, etc. – were more vulnerable if someone was socially cruel to them. It's likely that the cumulative effect of that trauma was important.

Notes

1. Naylon, K. (2014). What jealousy made me do. *Happen Magazine* (October8).http://www.match.com/magazine/article/6823/What-Jealousy-Made-Me-Do.

2. Pines, A.M. and Bowes, C.F. (1992). Romantic jealousy. *Psychology Today* (March 1). http://www.psychologytoday.com/articles/200910/romantic-jealousy.

3. Notable exceptions are one-time events that are so severe that they can cause real psychological damage, such as wartime situations or being a victim of a sexual assault.

4. Hale, R., Fox, C.L., and Murray, M. (2017). "As a parent you become a tiger": parents talking about bullying at school. *Journal of Child and Family Studies* 26 (7): 2000–2015. https://doi.org/10.1007/s10826-017-0710-z.

Chapter 5
Myth #4
Kids who are small and physically weak are targeted for bullying.

The footage is very unsettling. An amateur video shot in 2004, it shows a middle-aged man furiously beating a teenage girl with a belt. The man is in a state; he appears to use all his strength. Several years after it was shot, the video was posted online and went viral. Even in the United States, where most preschool children are still spanked periodically by parents,[1] many viewers seemed to regard the assault as abusive. Still, the most shocking part about this case wasn't even the beating itself, but the identities of the individuals involved. The man was – astonishingly – a family court judge named William A, and the girl he was beating was his then-teenage daughter, who suffers from ataxic cerebral palsy.

25 Myths About Bullying and Cyberbullying, First Edition.
Elizabeth K. Englander.
© 2020 John Wiley & Sons, Inc. Published 2020 by John Wiley & Sons, Inc.

Her physical vulnerability did not appear to constrain her father's fury at all. The girl, fearing her father's escalating temper, had surreptitiously made the video, and years later she was the one who subsequently released it.

In the flurry of media coverage that followed the video's release, few in the press defended Judge. Reporting from the *Today Show* on the case,[2] host Matt Lauer described how unnerving even seasoned newsroom journalists found the footage. Defensive in the face of an avalanche of revulsion, the judge downplayed the violence of his behavior. He told a Corpus Christi television station that the video makes the beating look "worse than it is" and asserted that although he had lost his temper, he hadn't done anything other than "discipline my child." His justifying self-defense seemed weak; but then, anyone would have found it challenging to defend the footage given the degree of violence used and the girl's disability.[3] The public may also have found the behavior incredible given the nature of his profession as a judge: in the course of a routine day, he might advise about parenting skills or render case decisions in loco parentis.

Apart from his job, in many other ways this appeared to be a very typical abuse case. The victim – his daughter – felt powerless, at least compared to her father. She later described him as a troubled man who routinely abused his family psychologically or physically; she saw her mother, her sister, and herself as readily available targets who were always subservient toward their patriarch. Like many other victims, she viewed the abuse as a cruel power play that exploited her inability to fight back. The Judge didn't see the situation in the same way. He felt it was *his daughter's behavior* that prompted the attack, and thus she was responsible. His daughter, in contrast, seemed to feel that her father beat her simply because he could.

Fortunately, bullying typically involves less extreme aggression, but it operates using very similar psychological dynamics. Bullying, like physical abuse, has always been a cruel exercise whereby the powerful prey on the vulnerable; but it's also a behavior that has become steadily less physical in recent years. Decades ago, researchers noted that small, weak boys were prime targets of bullying (a fact that every schoolchild also knew). Even today, parenting advice often uses cases of physically small boys as examples of victimization.[4] Photographs and artistic depictions of bullying still regularly show a small child being manhandled by a larger boy; and, as I pointed out in a previous chapter, physical injury is still cited as a warning sign of bullying.

But the fact is that bullying has largely shifted to a psychological phenomenon, and this change of weaponry has widened the bully's scope of possible targets. If you're not looking to beat someone up, there's not much point in confining yourself to a physically weak target. There are, however, many possible sources of *psychological* vulnerability. Using psychological tactics doesn't mean bullying and cyberbullying are no longer expressions of contempt and superior power; it simply means that when bullies and cyberbullies seek a vulnerable target, there are options far beyond physically weakest classmates.

Take Judge A' daughter as an example. Just as she saw her family's docility as a critical factor enabling her father's behavior, targets of bullying often point to their own psychological powerlessness as one reason for their victimization. In addition to traditional sources of defenselessness (like a small physical stature), signs of a psychological disinclination to fight back seem to increase vulnerability. Understanding this isn't the same thing as blaming the victim. We've long noted that a small stature might make a child more vulnerable to physical bullying; similarly, other characteristics may make a child more or less desirable as a target, from a bully's perspective. In a study of 453 teens I conducted in 2013, targets of bullying saw a characteristic tendency to back down and not assertively defend themselves as the most common reason for being victimized – not a lack of physical strength. A related possibility was that sometimes the victim wasn't personally unassertive but belonged to a group that was routinely targeted because of its perceived powerlessness. The makeup of high- and low-power groups or cliques can certainly vary from school to school; generally speaking, though, more powerful groups tend to be those associated with high-status sports, and less powerful cliques are often special education children or students who self-identify or are identified by peers as gay, lesbian, bisexual, or transgender. A number of studies have found that LGBTQ students are disproportionately targeted by bullies, and other research has found similar patterns for special needs children.[5,6]

But one's personality or group isn't the only point of vulnerability. Targets of bullying often cite their looks or, more specifically, their *weight* as the underlying cause of their defenselessness. Today, a child's weight may be their most vulnerable physical characteristic. Almost one-third of the victims in my research felt that their appearance increased their susceptibility to bullying. Another study found that weight is such a sensitive topic that even normal-weight children were sometimes bullied for being too "fat" (and so, predictably, were overweight children).[7] In my own research, overweight teens are at higher risk of peer cruelty, especially when there are "multiple, ongoing, repetitive episodes" (15% report this, versus 10% of regular-weight teens). They may be bullied more, but they don't seem to experience more of the milder, single-incident, random callous remarks or acts from their peers (67% of overweight teens and 69% of normal-weight teens report that).

It's not hard to see why kids today report being targeted because they belong to a vulnerable group, have a less confident personality, or don't have picture-perfect looks. But again, I'm not victim-blaming; even kids who are assertive, picture-perfect, and popular can become victims these days, because digital interactions can inject an element of vulnerability into any social power-play. Any rhyme or reason that dictates a bully's choice of victim in school is lacking online. Use of digital technology quite simply produces its own vulnerability. Any user, no matter what their traditional social status, can theoretically find themselves unable to defend themselves online. An online victim may be an acquaintance, a stranger, a school rival, or even a school bully. Any attack can feel amplified, so that even careless remarks can take on enormous significance. Misunderstandings, which can be rife online (where tone of voice and facial expressions often don't accompany messages), can produce a wellspring of cruelty and retaliation.

Peers who might not dare to attack in person can be much bolder online, where they don't have to face their targets. Bullies can attack anonymously, keeping their identities hidden, and this can be particularly intimidating and frightening for a target. In my 2011 study of 20 766 schoolchildren, anonymity seemed to be used in cyberbullying less and less often as children got older. Only 20% of the elementary-aged targets of cyberbullying in 2011 knew their online bully, but by high school, 73% of high schoolers knew the identity of their cyberbullies.[8] Since 2011, however, hugely popular apps and websites that encourage anonymous questions and answers, or the anonymous disclosure of secrets, have become very popular; and unsystematic studies of these apps suggest that when anonymous confrontation is encouraged, things get nasty pretty quickly. Digital technology hasn't only changed the types of vulnerabilities that bullies target; it's also changeable itself and may create new pockets of susceptibility here and there.

All of this suggests that it's not a myth to say that disadvantage can still be a key element in becoming a target of a bully. But although the type of disadvantages that bullies tend to target has clearly changed, other characteristics of bullying remain the same. Bullies continue to see targets as responsible for their own victimization. If you ask bullies how they choose their victims, they typically *don't* say they were seeking vulnerability. Just as Judge A did, they frequently point to their target's behaviors (blaming the victim) and their own anger (which they often see as justifiable and caused by the victim) as the motivation behind their bullying behaviors. In my research, both boys and girls who bullied saw anger as their main motive in about 70% of incidents. They characterized the bullying as an exchange with someone they didn't like or were mad at and *didn't* see it as a show of their own power or popularity – or as provoked by the target's physical or psychological characteristics. More than half of the bullies said they stopped bullying their target because they "stopped being mad."

Bullying might certainly be related to anger – anger can definitely exacerbate someone's cruelty – but if these behaviors were really just about being angry with a peer, then no particular victim typology would emerge. You can get mad at anyone, potentially; but choosing to only (or mostly) attack those who are vulnerable in some way suggests premeditation, not simply impulsive anger (or, at the very least, some combination of the two). But maybe kids who engage in bullying are simply citing anger as a motive because it's more socially acceptable than telling a researcher that they're targeting someone because of their popularity, their weight, their ethnicity, their sexuality, or other such characteristics. I was interested in trying to figure out if bullies really saw justifiable anger (and not social power) as their motive, so I decided to compare those who bullied repeatedly with others who admitted that they had committed a milder, occasional, mean remark or act. I asked both to describe their callous behaviors; then I examined their answers to see if they denied or admitted that what they had done was wrong.

The kids who were occasionally mean were more likely to agree with statements like "I wasn't thinking" or "what I did wasn't ideal." They admitted that their behavior was fundamentally wrong, but they tried to minimize the wrong. Repeated bullies were different, though – they were more likely to say that their behavior was "understandable and justified" or that they had "no other options" – attitudes suggesting that they saw themselves as largely devoid of wrongdoing. It's hard to know how sincerely and deeply they believed themselves to be justified, but if they were simply being mean *back*, why would their "tormenters" so frequently be such vulnerable peers? It doesn't add up. Even so, it's probably not always the case that bullies are out-and-out liars who are cynically trying to validate their repeated cruelty. Having talked and thought about anger as their motive, they may truly come to believe that their behavior is justifiable.

And there's another possibility. Research begun decades ago has found that children who are continuously aggressive tend to misinterpret neutral situations as hostile attacks. Most girls might see an ex-boyfriend's new girlfriend as someone who just likes him; but a more aggressive girl might believe that the new girlfriend's motivation is first and foremost to deliberately humiliate her. Under those circumstances, she might come to believe that any "retaliation" is totally justified, even if others think that she's the instigator. But again and again, we're drawn back to the fact that some kids – like LGBTQ or overweight youth – are far more likely to be targets. A tendency to misconstrue events as hostility can therefore only be part of the answer. Bullies today are clearly not confining themselves to physically weak victims; but they're hunting for vulnerability, all the same.

To-Do for Myth #4: Kids who are small and physically weak are targeted for bullying.

We know that vulnerable children are indeed targeted, but it's also often the case that children who are cruel don't see that as the rationale for their meanness. They may actually have a difficult time seeing their behavior the way others see it, and they can be focused on their own anger and their attempts to justify it. Thus the task is twofold: to help them see their spite as others do, and to clarify that even if they can't, open contempt or cruelty is never OK.

When children engage in cruel behaviors or show naked contempt toward their peers, we also need to acknowledge anger when it is present – but then draw the line clearly between feelings and behaviors. It's always OK to feel whatever you feel; but it's not always OK to act upon those feelings. We also need to promote the values that being kind to others and protecting those who are more vulnerable are always called for and always appropriate.

How can we use this data to help targets? Many programs exist that help – or purport to help – children become more self-confident and assertive. When they work, these

(continued)

(*continued*)

can help. But they certainly don't work for all children, and even if they did, some vulnerabilities are hard to avoid (e.g. belonging to a certain group, or using digital technology). But it's worthwhile to help children accomplish goals that can promote their self-confidence (for example, by mastering a musical instrument, or practicing enough to shine if they're athletic, or getting a new job or achievement in school). The accomplishments that have the most impact on children's self-confidence are those that they themselves really value; so if they have zero interest in playing the piano, forcing the skill may not help much. On the other hand, making the high school soccer team when they have real passion for the sport can be positively edifying.

Notes

1. UNC School of Medicine. (2010). Corporal punishment of children remains common worldwide, UNC studies find. http://www.med.unc.edu/www/newsarchive/2010/august/corporal-punishment-of-children-remains-common-worldwide-unc-studies-find.
2. NBC, msnbc.com, and news services. (2011). Judge's daughter: hope beating video gets him help. MSNBC. http://www.nbcnews.com/id/45135221/ns/us_news-crime_and_courts/t/judges-daughter-hope-beating-video-gets-him-help/.
3. Adams subsequently released a public statement in which he acknowledged the seriousness of cerebral palsy but denied that his daughter was physically disabled. http://extras.mysanantonio.com/pdf/JudgeAdamsstatement.pdf.
4. E.g. Peters, R. (2005). How to help keep your kid from being bullied. Davidson Institute. http://www.davidsongifted.org/db/Articles_id_10335.aspx.
5. GLSEN: Gay, Lesbian and Straight Education Network. (2009). National school climate survey: nearly 9 out of 10 LGBT students experience harassment in school. https://files.eric.ed.gov/fulltext/ED512338.pdf.

6. Lindsay, G., Dockrell, J., and Mackie, C. (2008). Vulnerability to bullying in children with a history of specific speech and language difficulties. *European Journal of Special Needs Education* 23 (1): 1–16. https://doi.org/10.1080/08856250701791203.

7. Puhl, R.M., Peterson, J.L., and Luedicke, J. (2013). Weight-based victimization: bullying experiences of weight loss treatment-seeking youth. *Pediatrics* 131 (1): e1–e9. https://doi.org/10.1542/peds.2012-1106.

8. Englander, E. (2012). Research findings: MARC 2011 survey grades 3-12. Massachusetts Aggression Reduction Center, Bridgewater State University. http://webhost.bridgew.edu/marc/MARC%20REPORT-Bullying%20In%20Grades%203-12%20in%20MA.pdf.

Chapter 6
Myth #5
The most important thing is what they did to you.

C ould your child's teacher be trying to kill you? In 1999, a biologist at Eastern Connecticut State University published a paper warning educators that giving a test could, quite simply, kill their students' grandparents. Mike Adams analyzed 20 years' worth of data and noticed a significant relationship: a student's grandmother was more likely to die right before midterm exams than any other time in the school year. What's more, if a student wasn't doing well in the class, then the grandmother was at an even *greater* risk of dying. Grandmas of failing students were 50 times more likely to perish! The absurd (and very funny) conclusion was that giving an exam appeared to lead directly to these untimely deaths. Adams' tongue-in-cheek paper was meant to demonstrate how easy it is to misjudge the cause of an event; and it was pretty effective. The data was real, but the conclusions were false. Exams and dead grandparents were correlated, but one didn't cause the other.

25 Myths About Bullying and Cyberbullying, First Edition.
Elizabeth K. Englander.
© 2020 John Wiley & Sons, Inc. Published 2020 by John Wiley & Sons, Inc.

Unfortunately, it's not always so easy to figure out if correlated events cause each other. There are plenty of possible cause-and-effect relationships that seem plausible. Are more babies born nine months after a blizzard? Does eating sugar exacerbate a cancerous growth? Do cold mothers cause autism? David Hume (the Scottish philosopher) speculated centuries ago that humans consistently try to see simple causal relationships because it's the way we make sense of the world. Many times, drawing those conclusions is relatively simple and reasonably accurate; at other times, it's more complicated. You can probably guess where I'm going with this. What are the critical factors that make an act of social cruelty truly hurtful? There are plenty of correlations, but it's not always easy to know which factors are important in causing trauma.

Let's start by considering how adults typically handle reports of social cruelty. The first thing we ask kids when they tell us that someone is being mean to them, is: *what did they do to you?* That's obviously not a pointless question. Clearly, it's critical to ascertain if an incident is one where someone's safety or life is in danger. Threats, violence, and sexual harassment are all examples of situations where the cruel behavior itself is of paramount importance in deciding how to respond. Imagine that your son reports that he was threatened at school. If the aggressor said he was planning to bring a gun to school the next day, you'd spring into action, and rightfully so. On the other hand, what if the threat was simply, "Do what I ask or I won't like you anymore"? In that case, you'd be much less likely to set off the alarms. But a lot of bullying and cyberbullying isn't as clear as that. Once we know it's not a more extreme situation that involves physical threats, violence, or sexual harassment, how important is it to know if a child rolled their eyes or ignored your son? In these more typical cases, *what they actually did* might not be of paramount importance, but the situation could still be serious. If your child's been a chronic victim of bullying, you shouldn't brush aside even seemingly minor acts. Asking *what they did* isn't good enough. We need a better way to judge the potential severity of a mean action.

In 2018, I conducted a study where I tried to sift through the characteristics of cruel online acts to figure out what characteristics predicted a negative outcome. It was clear to me that the same action could sometimes evoke totally different reactions from a target. Let's say that someone rolls their eyes when you get an answer wrong in class. In some situations, you truly might not care; in others, the action could really sting. So if it's not always the act itself that determines the impact, what does? Particularly in the case of online slights, it can be hard to figure out why one cruel act hurts, and why the same act sometimes doesn't.

I started this analysis by separating cyberbullying actions into "severe" and "not severe" categories. An example of a "not severe" category would be a friend posting a mildly embarrassing photo. Imagine that your friend takes a picture of you while you're laughing – the picture shows you with your mouth wide open. It's not a terrible picture, but it's not a flattering one, either. You probably wouldn't choose to post it yourself. Maybe your friend doesn't really think this through; he or she doesn't intend to embarrass you – they just post the picture because it looks sort of funny. And indeed, it is sort of funny. Mildly embarrassing too, but not a big deal. That would be an example of an online action that's negative but not seriously so.

On the other hand, imagine that someone takes a picture of your head and Photoshops it onto a pornographic image; then they post the picture online and show it all around the school on their phone. They do it maliciously, hoping to utterly humiliate you and hurt you as much as possible. That would definitely be a "severe" incident.

The first question I considered was whether the nature of the incident really predicted how hurtful it was. Is it worse to be the victim of a severe incident, rather than a mild one? Of course it is; but only sometimes. What I found in this research was that the "severe" incidents were more traumatic, but other factors were even more important in predicting impact. For example, the single biggest factor in determining impact wasn't whether the incident was severe or minor; instead, it was whether the target of the mean online act was also having social problems in school. In other words, the kids who were being targeted by bullies in school and online were much more vulnerable to online cruelty in general, whether it was minor or severe. The kids who weren't being targeted in school and who only experienced this one mean online act were much less impacted overall. In the middle were the kids who weren't being targeted at school but who had endured repeated attacks online. It seems, in other words, that context is key. If you're feeling pretty good socially, if you have good friends, and you're not the target of a bully, then you're likely able to endure a certain level of attack, either online or in school. On the other hand, if you're feeling pretty vulnerable, even a mild attack can be very hurtful.

Consider the differences here. If a subject reported that they were attacked only once online, and they weren't being bullied in school, then a more serious event increased the emotional impact by 12%. On the other hand, if they were also being bullied in school, the emotional impact was increased by 20% or more. So when we ask *what did they do to you*, we're not wasting time, but we may need to follow up with questions about the context. For example, we could ask *what did they do to you* and *what else is going on with you? Did this happen just this once, or is it part of a larger pattern in which you're being targeted by others?*

All of this makes sense when you think about how we assess more traditional bullying. Generally speaking, we ask if social cruelty in school is repeated (or has only happened once); if it's intentional (versus accidental or thoughtless); and if there's a power imbalance. These factors are, essentially, considering the context of an unkind act. What this new research suggests is simply that online cruelty is no exception to this rule.

To-Do for Myth #5: The most important thing is what they did to you.

The reality: What's important is both what they did to you and the context in which they did it.

You and your kids can practice taking context into account when you're considering the cause of what's hurtful and what's not. For example, you can use local or news cases to discuss context with your kids. Think about asking questions like these:

- Does it make a difference if the person being cruel to you is a friend, versus someone you barely know?
- I suspect that this wasn't the first time these two people had a problem with each other. What do you think?
- I know that just a look can seem very minor, but what if there are other problems going on? Couldn't that make it seem like just part of a big, negative pattern?

Chapter 7

Myth #6
Cyberbullying is just like bullying, only on the computer.

Wherever someone bullies, the elements are essentially the same: it's a more powerful person who repeatedly wages a campaign of cruelty against a target. But online conversations can sometimes be a square peg that doesn't fit well into a round hole. Take the case of Alanah Pearce, a young Australian video game reviewer who was the target of some pretty cruel and frightening remarks online. Like many people who blog or post online regularly, she sometimes receives a weird or nasty message. That's just part of working online. The standard advice in such cases is to ignore any threats; but after receiving several explicit rape threats (a particularly venomous and upsetting variety of

25 Myths About Bullying and Cyberbullying, First Edition.
Elizabeth K. Englander.
© 2020 John Wiley & Sons, Inc. Published 2020 by John Wiley & Sons, Inc.

intimidation), Alanah decided to respond. She didn't know what she would discover about the people who threatened her, but she certainly didn't expect to find that the putative would-be rapists weren't even men at all. To her astonishment, she discovered that several of these threats were coming from very young (even prepubescent) boys.

Alanah decided to take an old-fashioned approach. She looked up and notified the mothers of several of the boys who had threatened her online. At least one of them responded swiftly – and soon, Alanah received the boy's handwritten apology.

Is what happened in this case *bullying*? Or, more accurately – was it *cyberbullying*?

In the digital realm, it can be tough to fit behaviors into the criteria we set for bullying in person. Consider the characteristics of bullying: the behavior needs to be intentional, repeated, and impactful; and a bully is someone who has more power than the victim does. There's no doubt that a digital rape threat is egregious and repugnant, as well as being potentially an extremely hurtful act. It can even be terrorizing. Any recipient would be justifiably upset. But what was the intention of those young boys? Was the incident "repetitive"? These are harder questions to answer when the communication is online. Alanah doesn't think the boys intended to rape her, or even to scare her; she thinks their intention was to get her attention and possibly to show off for friends. Let's be clear: none of that excuses what these boys did. What happened online to Alanah was repugnant, very hurtful, and possibly criminal. It was a very serious wrongdoing, but it may not have fit the criteria for *bullying*.

It's important to remember that not everything cruel is bullying, and sometimes exceptionally cruel acts aren't bullying. Nowhere is this truer than online. This isn't an attempt to minimize anyone's behavior; it's an attempt to be clearer about what is and what isn't bullying per se. In the field, I see a lot of cases that don't fit a clear definition. If a teen receives a piece of gossip about someone and then forwards it to others, does that make the original sender a bully? Or is the child who forwards the rumor – but who didn't write it to begin with – the bully? Some digital cases seem more straightforward. When a child starts a "We Hate Jason" group online, posts rumors there about Jason, and continually encourages others to join the group, that seems pretty clearly to be intentional, repetitive, etc. But more often than not, the situations I run into in "real life" don't easily fit the mold. Instead, all too often I see the term *bullying* used in response to the target's level of hurt, instead of examining the intention and actions of the presumed bully. (Back in Chapter 1, I discussed how overusing the term *bullying* actually leads to its disempowerment.)

Not precisely fitting into the "bullying" mold is only one way that digital cruelty can be very different from the bullying that happens between kids at school. There are also important differences in how people perceive and understand communications when they're using digital technology.

Let's start with the most obvious examples. Misunderstandings are rife online. Digital messages, often in only brief bits of text, lack all the texture of in-person or phone conversations – the tone of voice, facial expressions, body language, and other details that convey emotion and context. Even adults often forget how easy it is to misconstrue messages absent this type of information. Recently, a New York schoolteacher who was trapped in a boring meeting texted his wife, asking her to "Call in a bomb threat." He added "ha ha" in the next message, but it was just a little too late, as his panicked wife had already phoned the police to report a bomb at the school.[1] The "ha ha" addendum was pretty important, as it turned out, to avoid exactly the misunderstanding that ensued. At the end of this chapter, I'll discuss a technique I use to discuss the issue of misunderstandings with kids.

Another way cyber-communication is different is due to the effect called *disinhibition*. To put it simply, people say stuff online that they would never say in person, and it's easy to see examples in the comment section of virtually any news story or blog. When communicating using digital technology, users can be much more self-focused; since the logical focus of their attention – the person they're speaking to – is physically absent, they may turn more of that focus inward and, momentarily, forget that another person is involved. Were the young boys who threatened Alanah Pearce really focused on *her* reaction? Or were they more interested in showing off for each other?

Emotions can also be experienced differently in digital environments. For example, much of what is discussed online is written down in black and white, which enables a user to read comments and discussions repeatedly. Envision what a string of text messages looks like, versus a conversation in person. During a traditional conversation, every statement is essentially gone as soon as it's spoken. But a digital string is there for the user to read and re-read, over and over, and this repetition can lead to a big emotional impact. The impact of repeatedly reading about feelings can change how intensely a user experiences an emotion that's being expressed online. I studied this once by having subjects in a study read either one or five text messages about their feelings; the ones who read more text messages rated themselves as more emotional. This is probably due to an effect known as *cognitive priming*, in which users can experience an intensification of their feelings when they repeatedly message back and forth with friends about their emotional state. Feeling a little upset? Text with your friends about it for a while, and you may begin to feel positively angry. *Priming* can easily happen in digital environments because of the repetitive nature of online exchanges, and it's one reason emotions can easily get out of control when people communicate through messaging or posting.

All of these factors mean that digital technology can skew what we feel, what we say, and how it comes across, so what happens in communication online can be very different from the types of communications that happen in person. Furthermore, there are types of social conflict, harassment, and bullying that appear to *only* happen online. One of these is coerced or pressured sexting. Although sexting is often conceptualized as a possibly misjudged but strictly voluntary (i.e. fun) activity, a disturbing proportion of sexters report that their adolescent sexting activities were at least partially the result of persistent and negative pressure from peers. Another type of cyberbullying communication that may only happen online is something I'm calling Factitious Digital Victimization.[2] In the past, a variant of this has been termed *self-cyberbullying* or *digital self-harm*. These behaviors are when a person uses digital technology to claim – falsely – to be a victim. It can be milder, like simply "going along" with others who are reporting victimization; or it can be more extreme, for example, when a user falsely sets up an alternate persona online, which they then use to cyberbully their "real" identity. Although about 15–20% of teens will admit to some type of Factitious Digital Victimization, most don't report the more extreme actions. Interestingly, this was originally thought of as a way to falsely report being cyberbullied; but in my 2017 study, most kids who engaged in this behavior reported that they had falsely claimed to be bullied in school – not cyberbullied.

To-Do for Myth #6: Cyberbullying is just like bullying, only on the computer.

Here's an exercise I often use with kids and professionals. What does the spoken phrase "I'm not mad" mean? Accompanied by an angry tone, it clearly means *I AM mad*. Accompanied by a friendly tone, its meaning is more straightforward – you're truly not mad.

Imagine the phrase typed or written in different ways. How does a period at the end change the tone of the phrase? How does the message change if you use all capitals? Does a "smiley face" emoticon change the message?

The purpose of this conversation isn't to have definitive answers. The "blushing face" emoticon can have different meanings for different people. The purpose of the exercise is to encourage kids to begin thinking about the tone of a conversation, and how much information the tone conveys.

Notes

1. Barreto, M. (2014). Teacher's text dangerously misunderstood. AOL. http://www.aol.com/article/2014/10/07/teachers-text-dangerously-misunderstood/20973830.

2. Howells, K. (1995). Factitious victimization: a forensic variant of Munchausen's syndrome? *The Journal of Forensic Psychiatry* 6 (3): 601–605.

Chapter 8
Myth #7
Bullying and cyberbullying are separate problems.

More than 25 years ago, when I was still a student, my father phoned me out of the blue one day to ask why on earth I had bought a motorcycle – and had done so using his credit card, to boot. I remember his voice revealing equal parts skepticism and indignation, since (as he knew) I'd never driven a motorcycle, I'd never revealed the slightest intention to own one, and I was, in fact, much too cautious to ever do so. I assured him that I didn't even know his credit card number, and reminded him that I hadn't the faintest interest in owning a motorcycle. We immediately suspected fraud – and pretty audacious fraud, at that. Because those were more innocent times, I was genuinely appalled

25 Myths About Bullying and Cyberbullying, First Edition.
Elizabeth K. Englander.
© 2020 John Wiley & Sons, Inc. Published 2020 by John Wiley & Sons, Inc.

to discover that someone would just buy an item of that magnitude using another person's credit card. The eventual explanation that came to light for the $7000 charge from a motorcycle shop was relatively less well-known in those days: of course, my dad's credit card number had been stolen. Back then, we were accustomed to thinking about theft as more of a hands-on crime, but no one came near him, or picked his pocket, or asked him to stick up his hands. The thief was never caught.

Today we know that stealing takes place both in person and online. In general, though, it's one of those offenses that tend to occur *either* in person or online but not often simultaneously in both arenas. When we think of stealing in person, perhaps it's about someone being mugged or having their house burgled. Online, their identity may be stolen using details from social media, or perhaps a credit card number is inadvertently revealed by a store. A thief might never come near you in person but might go on a shopping spree on a website (perhaps even one that sells motorcycles).

Is bullying the same type of offense – something that happens either in school or online, but not in both places simultaneously? Certainly our use of language seems to assume some type of impenetrable barrier between the two realms. In 2018, when I studied children who were bullied, slightly less than half reported that no adult (even their parent) ever asked if any part of the problem was occurring through social media or other digital communications. The reigning assumption seems to be segregation. Researchers and experts in bullying prevention often debate the comparative impact of bullying and cyberbullying, as though they seldom intersect and are so distinct that social cruelty at school will have no impact on how social cruelty online felt (or vice versa).

It's not only the *place* where bullying happens that's often thought to involve two distinct areas; the *people* who bully may be thought of as two unrelated groups as well. We all know that bullying at school happens between kids who know each other. In the case of girls, bullying often happens between girls who are (or were) actually friends. (That's one of the reasons bullying between girls may be more harmful than bullying that happens between boys.)

But although bullying is part of a dynamic in an existing relationship, cyberbullying is often seen as something that's done by strangers who may live on the other side of the world. It's true that some of the worst cases of cyberbullying depicted in media stories do involve strangers who aren't local. A young girl named Amanda Todd, in a heartrendingly tragic case, committed suicide after a stranger convinced her to bare her breasts to him and then subsequently revealed the picture on social media after she refused his attempts to blackmail her. Teenager Megan Meier also heartbreakingly committed suicide after meeting a stranger on the Internet who posed as a friendly boy and learning later that "he" (it was actually an adult female) had cruelly turned against her. These stories are hard to ignore, and they tap into a very primal fear: that our children might be doing fine, but if a deadly stranger comes along, all could be lost.

Given the salience of these issues – how much we read about these particular types of stranger-cyberbullies-someone and bullying-happening-in-school scenarios – it's not hard to see why many would assume that most bullying is one type or the other; perhaps cyberbullying has very little to do with what goes on in school.

But if you drill down a little deeper, you'll see a different dynamic, and not just in research findings. Even in media cases that involve a stranger online, the actions of peers at school (or just in person) often seem to play a part in determining outcomes. It wasn't just an online stranger who bullied Amanda Todd; her peers at school piled on, too – and viciously, by most accounts. Rebecca Sedwick, whose suicidal leap from an abandoned tower caught the world's attention, had named two local girls from her school as her tormentors, both in person *and* in cyberspace. Unlike stereotypes we may hold about cases involving a stranger on the Internet, it was alleged that these two had bullied her in school as well as online. Most cases involving suicide seem, upon closer examination, to involve multiple cruel incidents by people known to the victim, in multiple arenas. We learn things from these cases, without a doubt; we learn what kinds of problems are possible and how deep the wounds can go. But it's research data (not individual cases) that reveals to us how *frequent* different types of tragedies really are. Is Rebecca Sedwick's situation – being bullied across multiple situations, including both at school and online – the more typical experience? Or is bullying more like common theft, usually happening either in your house or online, but not in both arenas? If your child is cyberbullied, are the odds that the cyberbully is an adult predator, or is it more likely to be another child from their school?

Let's look at the segregation of bullying and cyberbullying first. There are incidents that only happen in school or only happen online. There are also incidents that happen in both arenas. The most common determinant of bullying's location seems to be the age of the child involved. Using data gathered in 2017–2019 on 2596 children aged 8–18, I compared the location of bullying between younger and older kids who were targets of bullies. Almost two-thirds (61%) of the youngest kids reported being bullied *only* in school, compared to 41% of the teens. But bullying online almost doubled between childhood and adolescence, involving 29% of the younger kids versus 58% of the teens. (A small minority of each age group reported being bullied *only* online.) These numbers suggest some separation of bullying and cyberbullying; if bullying takes place in only one setting, that setting is more likely to be in school if the target is very young. But as kids grow, bullying and cyberbullying are more and more likely to be intertwined with each other.

From a practical point of view, this makes sense. Digital communications are just another way to talk to and interact with friends. Any social interactions (positive or negative) that happen in school or online seem likely to be taken up again in the "other" location. Imagine that someone was being bullied in school and then, over the weekend, saw the bully at the mall. Wouldn't you expect that the bully to likely say something upon seeing their habitual target from school? Digital communications are no different. Bullying today might start only online, with the target wandering around school wondering which kid (or kids) are the mean ones. Or it might start in school and then quickly spread online, where other kids might talk about it or perpetuate it. Gossip that happens in one arena will often spread to the other. And earlier interactions color later ones;

if you've just spent the day being taunted at school, a mean text message feels much more toxic than one that appears on your cell phone screen without the context that was established earlier.

As kids grow, so does the relative influence of their digital interactions. But does this growing influence come largely from strangers, or from acquaintances? Most of the kids in my research who are in high school report that the people they usually interact with online are the same kids they know from "real" life. (Although much has been made of anonymity on the Internet [and it is an issue], it is employed as a weapon less often than many people think.) Even in the case of cyberbullying, most teens (about three-fourths) say that they know the identity of the cyberbully. Both girls and boys most often cite kids from their school as the person who's been cruel to them online. Other findings suggest that cyberbullying victims who know their abusers aren't isolated outliers, either. Consider almost any abuse case: the offender is usually someone the victim knows, and often someone the victim knows quite well.

An interesting question is why the specter of a stranger cyberbullying a child is so much more frightening than the idea of a familiar bully. In my research, kids express much more vulnerability when they're being bullied by a friend, versus by someone they barely know (an acquaintance). Research into other kinds of interactions finds similar patterns – it hurts more if the person who's being cruel to you is someone you know and trusted. In contrast, other research looking at how children respond to strangers who solicit them online finds less trauma. In one study, kids were asked how they responded to solicitations by strangers online who wanted to meet them in person. About two-thirds (66%) said they removed themselves from the situation or blocked the offender; another 16% warned the offender to stop; and 11% simply ignored the solicitations.[1] All this would suggest that it's not strangers we need to view as the biggest source of online trouble – it's the people we already know. Yet I consistently see resistance to that idea, and I think I understand why. Regarding all our friends and loved ones as potential abusers would, in effect, render those relationships meaningless. To some extent, we must put ourselves out on a limb and just trust that those we care about will care about us in return. Even so, parents everywhere can probably feel a little less anxious about the threat of an Internet Bogeyman, and perhaps pay a little more attention to the social relationships that are happening between children and their friends and acquaintances.

To-Do for Myth #7: Bullying and cyberbullying are separate problems.
The truth: bullying incidents often happen both in school and online. This is most true for teenagers.

What are the practical implications of these research findings? Those who are forewarned are forearmed. Let's talk to kids about cyberbullying, how it may often interact with bullying in school, and who is truly likely to be a cyberbully. There's a good chance your child already knows that most cyberbullies are other kids in school, and that what happens online intersects the social happenings at school. But even if they know all about these issues, talking about it still has value. When kids are aware of these pitfalls, they are less traumatized if they do happen, and every conversation increases thinking and awareness. The point isn't to teach kids to mistrust their friends; it's to make them aware that fights taken or begun online can get out of hand, and that there are ways to resolve problems with friends without launching a digital form of World War III.

Note

1. McPherson, T. (ed.) (2008). *Digital Youth, Innovation, and the Unexpected.* The John D. and Catherine T. Macarthur Foundation Series on Digital Media and Learning. Cambridge, Mass: MIT Press.

Chapter 9
Myth #8
Most adults cannot help kids with computer or Internet issues, since kids typically know more than they do.

I was trumped at the computer for the first time when my oldest was about five years old. A website we were trying to look at together just wouldn't load correctly. My little son suggested that I try a different browser; it was a great suggestion, and he was right. It worked.

It's always a surprise the first time your child knows something that you don't. And it's always been that way; but today, the difference is that there is one area of expertise in which virtually all children seem to show superiority – digital technology – and many seem to maintain that edge pretty consistently. Modern parenting is full of stories about children effortlessly outdoing their parents

25 Myths About Bullying and Cyberbullying, First Edition.
Elizabeth K. Englander.
© 2020 John Wiley & Sons, Inc. Published 2020 by John Wiley & Sons, Inc.

electronically and easily getting around feeble parental attempts to control technology: the parents who congratulated themselves for turning off the wireless Internet at 9 p.m. every night, only to find that their son simply used the neighbor's wireless network; the parents who took away their daughter's cellphone at night (something I've often advised parents to do), only to discover that the girl inserted her phone's SIM card (the chip that connects the phone to its network) into another, older phone, and continued texting her friends late into the night. Years ago, parents used to tell me that they thought an iPod was "just for music" and didn't realize kids could use it to text and talk to friends, just like a cell phone (as long as there was wireless Internet available).

What does kids' know-how about technology have to do with bullying and cyberbullying? Everything, it turns out.

Misunderstandings, which are widespread online, frequently lead to cyberbullying episodes. Cyber problems, in turn, can lead to problems in school – including bullying. In my research, kids who became victims of more serious issues online (such as being pressured or coerced into sexting) were more likely to have had a series of problems communicating with their peers in digital environments. Problems online and problems offline are profoundly related to each other in today's childhood and adolescence. Yet parents often feel that if their skills regarding digital technology aren't up to snuff, they can't be helpful for their kids in this regard.

The idea that kids are "naturally" skilled at using digital technology is an incredibly persistent belief. I've certainly heard often enough that kids "grew up with electronics," the implication being that we adults should throw up our hands and surrender. It's true enough that they're "digital natives," but growing up with one technology doesn't really account for why they're so proficient with other, newer technologies. A teen who grew up with computers might be understandably good with similar computers; but why do kids seem more skilled at adopting brand-new technologies that none of us have seen before? And it's not just a figment of your imagination. Researchers at the University of California found that younger people do possess certain traits that make them better at figuring out completely novel technologies. Basically, as we grow, the accumulation of everything we've learned makes us more cautious about learning new situations and jumping to quick conclusions. The California researchers came up with a novel approach to test the idea that younger brains have fewer problems learning new gadgets. They rigged a train that could be started or stopped using traffic lights, but they reversed the lights so that green indicated STOP and red indicated GO (the opposite of our traffic lights). Then they asked college students and preschoolers (four or five years old) to learn the new system. The younger children quickly learned how to control the trains, but the older teens found it much more difficult. Their life experience associating green as the GO color made it more difficult for them to learn that red was the new GO color. Life experience helps us cope, but it can also hinder our learning, especially when it comes to new and different situations or objects. For the little children in the study, their *lack of life experience* freed them to learn new causal relationships quickly, and they were more easily able to apply those relationships to a new environment.

Sound familiar?

The younger and more inexperienced you are, the better you may do when it comes to learning new technology. Sometimes, I think that adults don't mind it when kids know more – in fact, it can make us proud of our kids. But when it comes to digital technology, observing their ease with it can actually lead us to two erroneous conclusions: first, that being *comfortable* with technology is the same thing as being *knowledgeable* about all the technical and social issues related to technology; and second, that as the "lesser-skilled group," we parents have no role in helping kids learn to use technology. Neither of these conclusions is necessarily true, and both of them can lead adults to relinquish their guiding role.

When it comes to bullying and cyberbullying, though, the critical skill isn't how quickly you can learn a new app; it's how well you can interact socially – appreciating the nuances and considering the consequences – that really counts. And this is why you're not only relevant, you're critical, in helping your child think about what they're writing and messaging and posting online, and how it all might impact their relationships and their social lives.

Think about the issue this way: when it comes to communicating with technology, multiple levels of skills need to be developed.

Learning to use communications technology isn't like learning to use a dishwasher. To use a dishwasher, you just learn what buttons should be pushed; that's all there is to it. But using communications technology involves another ability on top of those basic how-to skills: understanding how communication *changes* in digital environments. You have to learn what to click on to send the message, but you also have to learn how to communicate what you're really trying to say, so you won't be misunderstood. You have to learn how to anticipate the impact of your communication and to pre-adjust it accordingly. You already know there's a difference between getting a paper letter, receiving an email message, and having a face-to-face conversation, even when they're all on the same topic. Why is a joke that's obviously funny in person somehow *not* funny (perhaps even offensive) when it's posted online? Why do conversations become more emotional when they're digital, and how much can you trust the intimacy you may feel when you're online talking to someone one-on-one?

Kids might be superior when it comes to learning how to use a device, but in my experience, adults are usually much better when it comes to understanding that talking in a digital environment is not the same thing as talking in person. So let's not throw the baby out with the bathwater. You may not be the best person to go to when a new gadget needs to be synced with data in the cloud; but if your son wants to make sure his online postings are getting across the intended message to a girl he's interested in, your insight may be exactly what he's looking for. If your daughter is hurt and baffled by a message from a friend that appears to be mean-spirited, it's your experience with having friends and the occasional misunderstandings that occur that can really help her. In my research, kids score pretty weakly on measures about how much they understand the impact of technological communications – not the how-to.

You may be thinking that understanding how to communicate what you really want to say is all about common sense and life experience; and it's true that these can take you pretty far on this issue. But there are also certain facts about communications in digital environments that research is just beginning to clarify for us. For example, several of my studies suggest that repetitive digital messaging

(messaging each other back and forth repeatedly about a topic of conversation) tends to increase emotional states instead of resolving them. Let's imagine that you're annoyed with your best friend, and you message other friends about your feelings; they are supportive, and that feels good. The problem is that reading and writing repeatedly about your annoyance can actually make your emotions intensify until you're feeling really mad – no longer simply annoyed. Many adults have the life experience to understand that when you're irritated with someone, the best and more reliable way to resolve the feeling is to talk with that person face-to-face. The times we've spent talking with others or chewing over the issue in our mind, in contrast with confronting and addressing the problem, have taught us the futility of taking easier but roundabout paths to resolution. When you're upset, there is no real substitute for talking in person.

Kids, though, don't benefit from all that life experience, so they're still looking for easier ways to feel better. They could, of course, talk face-to-face with friends for emotional support – and they do – but with digital means literally at hand, they may go for the fastest possible communication. You might know that it would be better for them to talk; but they may believe that texting friends for support is just as good. And it does feel good to have caring and encouragement from friends. What kids don't realize (and you may not, until right now) is that by reading and writing repeatedly about their feelings, they can end up feeling more and more frustrated. And if they're feeling increasingly upset, they may assume that the original source of their frustration is to blame. Kids aren't terribly likely to say to themselves, "Gee, this repetitive technology is really priming my emotions." Instead, they'll just be madder at their friend, who may not understand why their anger seems completely out of proportion to the issue at hand.

There are other ways that communication changes online, too. If you're sitting in a physically private space (like your own home), you're more likely to feel as though what you're doing is truly private and confidential (more on this in another chapter); and unless you're using a video-caller like Skype or Facetime, it's very easy to misunderstand what someone means, since you don't have the benefit of their facial expressions, their body language, or the tone of their voice. Without another person physically there during your conversation, it's easy to forget about focusing on their reactions (which you do instinctively when they're present); and you might over-focus, instead, on your thoughts about your own behaviors. So a young boy might forget that his blatantly misogynistic words are offensive to a girl, and might be thinking instead, "Am I appearing funny and cool?"

The key skill seems to be the understanding that using technology to communicate effectively isn't something you're born with; it's a skill you have to develop, and it usually means consciously suspending a lot of commonplace assumptions about communicating. For example: they won't always get that you mean something as a joke. Or: this may feel very intimate, but it's really not as private as it feels. Someone may not be right there with you, but they still have feelings; how will what you've written come across?

To-Do for Myth #8: Most adults cannot help kids with computer or Internet issues, since kids typically know more than they do.

Technology skills can be divided into two basic categories: how to use a device, and how to communicate using that device. A deficit in either set of skills can lead to cyberbullying or to thinking you're a victim of cyberbullying when you're not.

As a parent, you may not feel very capable when it comes to the first category of skills, but you are likely invaluable when it comes to the second set. Talk with your kids about situations they've seen or heard where someone misunderstood someone else; what happened, and are there better ways to handle these kinds of situations? Are there situations where technology is a good way to handle things, and situations where talking face-to-face is better?

Chapter 10
Myth #9
Bullying and cyberbullying stop after high school.

I had a pretty hard time in my first year. I got put into an all-girl flat and unluckily the girls who I were put with were really nasty. They would leave me out, ignore me and blank me every day. They would shout at me, gang up on me and felt I had nowhere to turn. In the end, I was able to move in with a nicer group of people.[1]

Charlotte, aged 20

He wrote a note on Facebook, left his college dorm, put his wallet and phone on the George Washington Bridge, and jumped. Soon after, in the middle of the night, came the phone call that every parent dreads – the police telling them that something terrible had happened to their child. For Joseph and Jane Clementi, that phone call came in 2010, waking them out of a deep sleep and revealing to them the awful possibility that their son had just jumped off the George Washington Bridge, presumably to his death.

25 Myths About Bullying and Cyberbullying, First Edition.
Elizabeth K. Englander.
© 2020 John Wiley & Sons, Inc. Published 2020 by John Wiley & Sons, Inc.

As the case unfolded, it became clear that their son Tyler's peers had been exposing his private life online, ultimately resulting in the humiliation that may have finally driven him to commit suicide. Tyler's college roommate had tweeted (sent out messages on Twitter, a social media site) about seeing Tyler "making out with a dude." After catching glimpses of the tryst with the clandestine use of a webcam, the roommate had invited others to a "viewing party" on a subsequent date – an online invitation that Tyler saw. The viewing party never happened, but the damage may have already been done. Tyler Clementi wasn't a vulnerable teen still in high school, and it wasn't another 15-year-old who allegedly tormented him online. Everyone involved in this sad case was older, attending Rutgers University. The last thing that Tyler Clementi allegedly saw before jumping off that bridge were posts and comments by others on the Internet, making fun of him.[2]

We think of bullying as a problem that ends after high school, but achieving legal adulthood didn't bring Tyler any assurances that his peers wouldn't be cruel, or that he would have somehow learned not to care. Being exposed as gay before feeling ready to announce one's sexual orientation is devastating at any age; but we tend to think that after surviving what some teens experience as the social gauntlet of high school, college students will have the capacity to withstand any social aggression. And if they cannot, it surely doesn't matter as much, since maturity presumably bestows on the adolescent bully a measure of increased thoughtfulness and consideration. Bullying is a behavior we tend to associate with immaturity and thoughtlessness.

But if you actually measure bullying and cyberbullying in college, you find that the problem most definitely exists and that targets are often still quite vulnerable. Approximately 26% of the college students I surveyed in 2018 reported having had an experience with harassment, bullying, cyberbullying, or similar problems with peers *while at college*. Some problems happen between roommates or classmates, or between young adult students who date each other. More than a third of the students I surveyed said they had had a problem with a dating partner, or with breaking up with a dating partner, while in either high school or college. In class, a student of mine wrote poignantly about her post-high school dating experiences:

I dated someone when I was 21 from another state. We lived a few hours away from each other and I made a similar mistake to Amanda Todd. I let him take photos of me that I wouldn't want anyone else to see, but thought I was in love and nothing bad could happen. Everyone can be naïve at times and that certainly was what happened in my situation. I thought that it was okay that he had the photos because we didn't get to see each other as much as we would like and that he loved me so he would never hurt me. I eventually broke up with him and then he started black mailing [sic] me. He would text me and message me saying that he would take those pictures and put it on websites to let the world to see. He told me if I didn't go see him that he would show everyone. I was so scared and didn't know what to do at first, that I went to see him and pretended to still like him so he would calm down.

Bullying, cyberbullying, and sexting in college don't come out of nowhere. In a 2014 survey, I found that the risk of having such peer problems in college was highest for students who also reported being victims of bullying and cyberbullying while in high school. More than a third of those high school targets – 43% – went on to be victimized similarly in college. In comparison, 21% of subjects who reported having fights with friends while in high school reported being bullied or cyberbullied while in college. It may be that the earlier bullying causes more emotional vulnerability that in turn makes college students easier targets. A study examining these factors directly found that college students who were bullied in high school might have more emotional struggles but not always more bullying victimization in college.[3] A similar study pointed out that students who were victims of bullying reported a lower quality of life.[4] This doesn't mean a bullying victim is doomed to a life of unhappiness, but it may mean they'll need a little more social support when they go to college or start a new job. It's also worth pointing out that bullying isn't only peer-to-peer; students who felt bullied by their high school teachers were also more likely to report feeling bullied by their college professors.[5]

Despite all this, it's important to keep in mind that bullying and cyberbullying victimization appear to decline during the college years. The preponderance of events in college still occurred online – more than two-thirds of incidents were either partially or wholly through digital means – but overall, the decline in frequency was obvious. People do grow up; targets often become more resilient, and offenders may become more mature or even more sensitive. But bullying and cyberbullying are problems that can persist into higher education and adulthood.

To-Do for Myth #9: Bullying and cyberbullying stop after high school.

For parents today, it can be tempting to heave a sigh of relief upon high school graduation and assume that the social drama of adolescence is largely over. But data suggests that it may continue, and it may be most likely to continue for those who struggled socially while still in high school. It's perfectly reasonable to discuss the ways in which socializing can improve after 12th grade: at college, there are many people to meet, and all of them are new; in a job, similarly, there can be a fresh start, socially speaking. But it's also prudent to keep talking with your young adult offspring as they navigate these newer waters to see how things are going socially and to make sure their family support is still there while they're trying out their wings.

Notes

1. Bullying UK. (n.d.). Bullying at university. Family Lives. https://www.bullying.co.uk/general-advice/bullying-at-university/ (accessed 5 December 2019).
2. Knapp, K. (2015). Family of Tyler Clementi visits Princeton, talks to Corner House student leaders about anti-bullying campaign. Planet Princeton.http://planetprinceton.com/2015/08/14/family-of-tyler-clementi-visits-princeton-talks-to-corner-house-student-leaders-about-anti-bullying-campaign.

3. Holt, M.K., Green, J.G., Reid, G. et al. (2014). Associations between past bullying experiences and psychosocial and academic functioning among college students. *Journal of American College Health* 62 (8), 552–560. https://doi.org/10.1080/07448481.2014.947990.

4. Chen, Y-Y. and Huang, J-H. (2015). Precollege and in-college bullying experiences and health-related quality of life among college students. *Pediatrics* 135 (1), 18–25. https://doi.org/10.1542/peds.2014-1798.

5. Marraccini, M.E., Weyandt, L.L., and Rossi, J.S. (2015). College students' perceptions of professor/instructor bullying: questionnaire development and psychometric properties. *Journal of American College Health* 63 (8), 563–572. https://doi.org/10.1080/07448481.2015.1060596.

Chapter 11
Myth #10
Cyberbullying is usually anonymous.

Cyber bullies can hide behind a mask of anonymity online and do not need direct physical access to their victims to do unimaginable harm. (Anna Maria Chavez)

Cyberbullying is Bullying. Hiding behind a pretty screen, doesn't make it less hateful, written words have power. (Anonymous)

It's easy to be mean when you're anonymous. There's a lot of people who wouldn't have the cajones to say in person what they do online. But you can't listen to somebody you don't even know. Opinions of your friends and family matter, but you can't listen to somebody who is nobody to you. (Brendan Dooling)
EdTechReview.com[1]

In 2014, one of the hottest new apps was a message-posting app called *Yik Yak*. Using Yik Yak, anyone could post a comment online that would be visible to anybody else using the app within 5 miles. The secret to Yik Yak's appeal wasn't in its visual design or its

25 Myths About Bullying and Cyberbullying, First Edition.
Elizabeth K. Englander.
© 2020 John Wiley & Sons, Inc. Published 2020 by John Wiley & Sons, Inc.

geographical range, though; it appealed because it didn't require users to log in or disclose their name or email address. In other words, it offered the lure of apparent anonymity. I say *apparent* anonymity because other identifying information (such as IP address[2] and geographical location) was still gathered about users, even if they didn't realize it was happening – and they didn't, by and large. A young football player I'll call J.C. found this out the hard way when he posted a threat on Yik Yak to blow up his school. Although he probably thought he was being funny, and he almost certainly believed his threat was untraceable, the identifying information that had been electronically gathered on him permitted police to pinpoint and arrest the young man. Yik Yak doesn't try to hide the fact that the app isn't truly anonymous, and its website did warn users outright that they shouldn't post threats without expecting repercussions. Still, many thought the site's pseudo-anonymity rendered users essentially able to post anything, about anybody – without consequences.

Yik Yak wasn't an oddity. Social media apps offering pseudo-anonymity have popped up periodically, and a number have become popular fads. It isn't difficult to imagine how a teen might find it entertaining to pose a question with no consequences or social rules inhibiting them. You'd be able to ask your friend why, year after year, she gives everybody those gross cookies for Christmas, when no one ever eats them. You could ask your cousin why he doesn't realize how horrible his haircut looks. You could tell someone you have a secret crush on them. More sinisterly, you could ask a friend you're mad at if he realizes what a dork he is and that no one really likes him. Messages on these apps aren't always innocently curious; anonymity can be, and is, used to hurt others. But plenty of people are attracted by the idea of being able to tell the world what a jerk their boss or their teacher can be, with no possibility of losing their job or getting in trouble as a result. Of course, as many cases have taught us, the perception of anonymity online is usually just that – a perception. J.C. is only one of many people who have stumbled into legal trouble through their IP addresses.

Anonymity was a hassle to achieve before the Internet, and that was probably a good thing. A quick glance through classic movies reveals the pre-electronics technique: to create an anonymous message, you had to cut words or letters out of a magazine, glue them on a page, and sneak over to your target's house in the dead of night to stealthily slip your message into the mailbox. Even typewriters could be associated with the letters they typed, and using the US mail system was out of the question unless you were willing to travel continents out of your way to mail a letter. It's clear that making anonymity easier (that is, digitizing it) has increased the appeal of being able to say anything or ask anyone any question easily, quickly, and without anticipating any backlash or repercussions. Still, we should be careful what we wish for; while technology has made this type of commentary a realistic possibility, the nasty downsides are palpable. Cyberbullying is only one possibility. Bomb threats like J.C.'s are an ongoing problem. The National School Safety and Security Services studied school threats over a six-month period and found that more than a third came in via social media, email, or text message.[3]

But the link between anonymity and cyberbullying is our particular interest here, and it has been speculated upon for years, even before the current trend toward hiding oneself online really gained traction. If a person perceives himself to be anonymous – that is, if they believe they cannot be identified or associated with their actions – then it seems they're more likely to behave in an illicit or antisocial way. Researchers at Gettysburg College followed a group of college freshmen over four points in time. They found that students who believed more strongly in their anonymity online were significantly more likely to engage in cyberbullying at a later point in time.[4]

This kind of study makes it tempting to conclude that if anonymity leads to more cyberbullying, then anonymity must be a major cause of cyberbullying. But the ability to be anonymous online may actually be an unusual impetus to bully, and other research suggests that many (maybe most) cases of cyberbullying may have nothing to do with anonymity. Think of it this way: if you were driving your car and the steering wheel came off in your hand, you'd almost certainly crash. So, the link between the steering wheel disconnecting and crashing is strong, but most crashes have nothing to do with a steering wheel malfunction. Similarly, we may see that anonymity is strongly linked to cyberbullying, but that doesn't mean anonymity one of the most *common* causes of cyberbullying.

Unfortunately, the strength of the connection between anonymity and cyberbullying has led to a general assumption that cyberbullies are cowards who usually hide their identities online. But some evidence contradicts that idea. First, the recent rise in anonymous apps hasn't resulted in a corresponding increase in cyberbullying – in fact, cyberbullying may have declined slightly in recent years. If anonymity online were a major cause of cyberbullying, then more opportunities to feel anonymous should have led to more cyberbullying. Second, several studies have suggested that most kids who experience remarks or actions online know the identity of their abuser. When I studied 451 teenagers in 2014 and 2015, I found that only 8% of the cyberbullying victims didn't know the identity of their bully. The other 92% said that they knew who was targeting them online. Just as with traditional bullying, more than half the time the online bully was a friend or a former friend. Another third of the victims identified the cyberbully as someone from school, albeit someone they didn't know very well. Girls, with their more intense social relationships, were more likely to identify friends or former friends as the source of their electronic misery. Boys, in contrast, were more likely to identify acquaintances from school. Other studies have similarly found that most victims of cyberbullying appear to know the identity of their bullies.[5]

How do we reconcile data like this with the popularity of anonymous apps like Yik Yak? First, it's important to remember that anonymity may encourage cruel or thoughtless remarks, but that doesn't mean most anonymous remarks are mean-spirited. The anonymous postings on Yik Yak are probably more often gossipy, sexualized, or bored than they are unkind. In other words, as I pointed out earlier, more use of anonymous apps doesn't necessarily mean that more cyberbullying is anonymous. I also think we simply notice anonymous cyberbullying more, not least because it can be much scarier. If your cyberbully is a mystery person, then walking through the school (or work) hallways can become an exercise in torturous intimidation. Any person strolling past, looking at you, even being nice to you might be the same person who is working hard to terrify and humiliate you. The stress of being unable to trust anyone, even friends, can be nerve-wracking. In the social pressure-cooker of adolescence, that fear may feel magnified.

Yet, overall, just like with bullying in person, cyberbullying appears to be a problem that usually happens *between people who know each other.* While anonymous cyberbullying does happen and can be very frightening, it seems to be the less likely type.

To-Do for Myth #10: Cyberbullying is usually anonymous.

The reality: Cyberbullies are often not anonymous, although youth who believe that they're anonymous online are more likely to become cyberbullies.

At first glance, there might not seem to be much of a "to do" that arises from this particular myth. After all, it's really about the fact that most cyberbullies aren't truly anonymous. But there may be a larger point worth thinking about. In today's digital world, kids can be easily fooled by marketing ploys into thinking that their Internet use is, in fact, anonymous. Once they think that, they may post things that can quickly get them into hot water. In contrast, it's a good skill to understand what an IP address is and why it means that true and total anonymity is rarely achieved online. An *IP* (Internet Protocol) *address* is a unique number that identifies a device. Every device that goes online has a unique IP address; so, for example, if you use your cell phone to call in a bomb threat, police will be able to figure out that you were the perpetrator by tracing the IP address of the threat back to your cell phone. Once a user understands what IP addresses are and how they always reveal who's sending a message, they won't be fooled into thinking that what they're doing online is untraceable and, therefore, not subject to social rules – or laws.

Notes

1. Gupta, P. (2016). 20 cyber bullying quotes that you must spread right now. EdTechReview. https://edtechreview.in/news/2326-cyber-bullying-quotes (accessed 5 December 2019).

2. An IP address (Internet Protocol address) is essentially a number that identifies any device that goes online. Anytime a user accesses an app or a webpage, their IP address is recorded and can be retrieved – which means the user can be identified.

3. Trump, K. (2014). Schools face new wave of violent threats sent by social media and other electronic means, study says. National School Safety and Security Services. http://www.schoolsecurity.org/2014/02/schools-face-new-wave-violent-threats-sent-social-media-electronic-means-study-says.

4. Barlett, C.P. (2015). Anonymously hurting others online: the effect of anonymity on cyberbullying frequency. *Psychology of Popular Media Culture* 4 (2): 70–79. https://doi.org/10.1037/a0034335.

5. Lapidot-Lefler, N. and Dolev-Cohen, M. (2015). Comparing cyberbullying and school bullying among school students: prevalence, gender, and grade level differences. *Social Psychology of Education* 18 (1): 1–16. https://doi.org/10.1007/s11218-014-9280-8; Varjas, K. et al. (2010). High school students' perceptions of motivations for cyberbullying: an exploratory study. *The Western Journal of Emergency Medicine* 11 (3): 269–273.

Chapter 12
Myth #11
Cyberbullying is the most emotionally devastating form of bullying.

S ome bad things are scary precisely because they *aren't* predictable. We fear events like car crashes because we can't ever truly know when or if they're going to happen, and there's nothing we can do to avoid them entirely. Even if we never drink and drive, always drive under the speed limit, and never drive on bad roads or in messy weather conditions, we're always partly at the mercy of other drivers, who may not be as careful. It's the unpredictability of the risk that makes it so frightening.

In 1918, the world experienced the worst flu pandemic ever recorded; a mind-bending 50–100 million people died (making it one of the most lethal events in human history). Flu is a disease that

25 Myths About Bullying and Cyberbullying, First Edition.
Elizabeth K. Englander.
© 2020 John Wiley & Sons, Inc. Published 2020 by John Wiley & Sons, Inc.

can range from mild to very serious, and it certainly killed people before 1918. But the flu that happened that year was different and much more frightening. Most flu targets the very young and the very old: it seeks out and is much more lethal for those vulnerable populations. But the 1918 flu was terrifying because it aggressively killed the young and the strong.[1] Several military bases – places full of strong, healthy young men and women – were among the most decimated. That made this flu different and much more alarming. Death is always sad, but it's more predictable when those who are already vulnerable become sick. It was the specter of a disease that could suddenly take down the healthiest among us that made it all the more frightening.

Like the flu of 1918, suicide is a dreadful event that is not necessarily predictable. It occasionally appears to happen without warning, but at other times, people who commit suicide have a history of depression and mental health challenges. Perhaps they've had some bad luck; maybe they've lost a job or come down with a terrible disease; or they've simply struggled with depression and anxiety for a long, futile time. In hindsight, we can sometimes see the factors that led someone to suicide.

Yet when suicide is associated with cyberbullying, it can feel more like the flu epidemic of 1918. Many parents fear that not only does cyberbullying happen out of the blue, but a well-adjusted, happy, healthy child or teenager may abruptly self-injure or even commit suicide because of it. This impression – that cyberbullying is so uniquely devastating that it can deliver a completely crippling blow – is probably the result of all the media stories we hear about or read that link suicide and cyberbullying. It's not unusual for the media to depict these stories as cases where cyberbullying took down children who were otherwise doing very well. Twelve-year-old Rebecca Sedwick committed suicide in 2013, and media reports about her often emphasized that her family thought she was doing well and did not know the extent of her social struggles with bullying and cyberbullying. Less emphasized was the fact that she had longstanding social problems, was very badly victimized by peers, had been cutting herself, and was almost certainly very depressed.

But the depiction of cyberbullying as a problem that can cut down even the healthiest young person builds cyberbullying up into a relentlessly scary bogeyman. While no parent wants to hear about their child being depressed, a suicide without any warning bells, based on peer activities that parents don't even know about, seems even worse.

Bullying can be scary for the same reason, but digital problems really lend themselves to this type of fear, precisely because parents often feel that they're barely treading water when it comes to keeping on top of what their children are up to online. If you feel uncertain about technology yourself, then how will you have conversations with your child about social problems like cyberbullying and how these might be affecting them? As an example, consider the father who once told me that his daughter had assured him not to worry about photos she posted on Snapchat because "they disappear." "What does it mean, they disappear?" he asked me. His sense that he didn't understand the technology put him in a bind. He couldn't feel reassured by her explanation, and yet he felt like he didn't know enough to question her assertion. (While parents often feel as though they shouldn't reveal that they don't understand a technology, in my experience this is not really a disadvantage. Let your child teach you. Kids love to be the expert! Don't forget to ask questions and bring up commonsense issues.)

Put together the idea that cyberbullying feels like it can be a lethal bolt out of the blue with a feeling that one lacks expertise in digital technology, and you can see why so many parents struggle with a profound sense of anxiety and helplessness. But it's important to know that this is not the reality of cyberbullying. It does *not* actually follow this pattern, at least not the vast majority of the time. While cyberbullying can be an unexpected social problem, it isn't always worse than traditional bullying, and suicide is an unusual outcome in either case.

Two firmly established research facts can help douse all this drama. First, although social problems can cause kids distress and even depression, cyberbullying isn't implicated any more strongly than are other types of social difficulties. Kids fight with friends;

they switch friends or groups of friends; they may bully or be bullied. They may become depressed or develop an anxiety problem. None of these problems are rare, and all of them can cause some or (occasionally) a lot of distress. Yes, many kids are hurt by social traumas; yet many kids are also resilient. Children can benefit enormously from the support they get from family and friends, and they can learn coping skills that help them deal with difficult social situations. In the scheme of things, when it comes to social stress and emotional responses, cyberbullying doesn't stand out as significantly worse or different than other social challenges. This doesn't mean cyberbullying doesn't hurt; but there's no compelling body of evidence demonstrating that it hurts significantly more than other harmful social interactions.

Second, when we look at the cases where cyberbullying *is* implicated in a suicide, we almost always see that the child in question was already struggling with depression and/or other emotional challenges. As I pointed out earlier, Rebecca Sedwick had a history of difficult peer relationships and self-injury. Amanda Todd, whose poignant online cry for help went viral after her death, was profoundly depressed by a series of stressors, including (but not limited to) cyberbullying before her suicide. Megan Meier, whose mother created a foundation in her honor after her post-cyberbullying suicide, had struggled with self-esteem issues, depression, and attention deficit disorder. The list goes on and on. There's little doubt that cyberbullying is associated with an increased risk of suicide.[2] But (and this is an important but) most children who are cyberbullied don't commit suicide. Suicide is a drastic step. It's when cyberbullying is piled on top of other problems – depression, impulsivity, dysphoria – that suicidal possibilities begin to creep out from the shadows.

So perhaps the relationship between cyberbullying and suicide isn't so much a direct line; maybe, instead, this indirect association tells us that we need a better understanding of how and when cyberbullying and bullying lead to problems like depression. We know that some kids are able to shrug off bullying and cyberbullying, while others are much more affected. Research done by me and by others has uncovered a few of the factors that seem to help kids be more resilient. When kids are able to talk with their parents and families about their troubles, resiliency rises; when their families are in the grip of problems like divorce or substance abuse, resiliency falls. When kids feel close to friends and feel they can count on them, resiliency rises; when they fight a lot with friends, resiliency falls. When kids feel like they have an adult at school whom they like and feel they can talk to, resiliency rises; when they feel isolated and alone, with no adult to talk to about their troubles, resiliency falls.

Social rejection isn't a rare or unusual event while growing up. Although it's an experience that most parents would love to spare their kids, there is no method for entirely avoiding social hurts. Instead of trying to build our kids a world where no one is ever mean to them, the trick may be to reinforce their mental health with social support from friends, families, and others, so that when and if a problem arises, they're resilient enough to handle it successfully.

To-Do for Myth #11: Cyberbullying is the most emotionally devastating form of bullying.

Weathering bullying and cyberbullying is all about social support, but not all children enjoy the same level of help and encouragement. If your family is coping with a stressful situation, you may feel as though you have little, if any, control over events. Having said that, it can be easy to become absorbed in problems and to forget how vulnerable these difficulties can make children feel. Even if your children appear to be handling a family problem well, take the time

(continued)

(*continued*)

to "check in" and see how they're feeling about life in general. Eat dinner with them, and ask how things are going at school and how their friends are. Talk while you're driving them somewhere in the car, or when you're on a train or a bus together. Ask about their friendships and their technology use, and don't worry if you don't understand the technology they refer to. Ask questions until you do understand what they're talking about, and use your life experience and common sense to question their assumptions.

For example: "I understand that you're saying Snapchat images disappear after a minute or two. But what would stop someone from making a copy of the image during the minute or two it's visible?"

What if your child's most pertinent struggle is with peers? It's all well and good to advise adults to encourage supportive friendships between children, but what if your child has few (or no) friends? Sometimes it's helpful to look for friends in unconventional places. Some children benefit greatly from having friends outside of school, even if they remain socially isolated at school. Consider encouraging friendships that form at camp, during after-school activities and sports, or from religious activities. Even friends online can be wonderfully comforting for isolated kids, but gently encourage such children to keep seeking in-person friends, too.

Finally, a socially isolated child can receive a lot of support from school adults. If your child doesn't feel supported socially by peers, ask the school counselor to let him or her know that they can come and talk whenever they need to. They may never take advantage of that offer, but just knowing that someone is there can make a big difference.

Notes

1. Wikipedia. (2019). Spanish flu. https://en.wikipedia.org/wiki/Spanish_flu.
2. John, A., Glendenning, A., Marchant, A. et al. (2018). Self-harm, suicidal behaviours, and cyberbullying in children and young people: systematic review. *Journal of Medical Internet Research* 20 (4): e129. https://doi.org/10.2196/jmir.9044.

Chapter 13
Myth #12
Bullies have emotional problems.

This girl used to torment me all through high school and middle school .... Of course I was miserable, and my dad would try to cheer me up. "Don't worry kiddo, one day she'll be working at a McDonalds and serving you fries."

A couple years after graduating high school I went to a Hardee's with my dad. And there was McDonalds behind the counter. So I go up to place my order and before I finish she says, "you don't remember me, do you?"

> *"Oh, I remember you."*
> *"Oh ... so, would you like fries with that?"*
> *"Why yes, yes I would."*
> *Way to go, dad. Called it 9 years in advance.*
> *—A user on Reddit, 2014*

The idea that bullies may flex their muscles but are ultimately doomed to be weaker than their victims, even if only in less-than-obvious ways, is a comforting one. Traditionally, bullies have been

25 Myths About Bullying and Cyberbullying, First Edition.
Elizabeth K. Englander.
© 2020 John Wiley & Sons, Inc. Published 2020 by John Wiley & Sons, Inc.

conceptualized as boys (usually) who are physically large and strong, but academically weak and psychologically stunted. They bully others because they secretly hate themselves, have poor self-esteem, and need to dominate socially to forget their own inadequacies. That stereotype has been depicted in dozens of books and movies.

It's a consoling cliché because it associates mean-spirited social dominance with psychological and cognitive problems that, in the long term, seem pretty likely to bring down a bully. Vengeance may elude you in school, but life will ultimately even the score. In other words, if you can get through high school, your bully will indeed be serving you french fries (even if only figuratively). And it hasn't only been the general public that has viewed bullies this way. Decades ago, researchers often described bullies as children who, inevitably, functioned very poorly. Their grades were bad. They disliked themselves. Other kids disliked them.

But even if we are secretly pleased with the idea of a maladjusted bully and the cosmic justice this seems to serve, researchers know today that many bullies just don't fit this stereotype. The fact is, some bullies are far from unpopular. They may actually be academically successful and social leaders in school and online. Certainly there are those who bully because of their own poor self-esteem; but equally certainly, others bully for other reasons. It can seem incredible to think the bullies might be popular: amazing because, first, a popular teen would seem to not need to bully; and second, it's hard to believe that other students would admire and look up to someone who bullies. But to help wrap your mind around this idea, consider what we know about what really impacts social status during pre-adolescence and adolescence. Researchers who study it find that social status is related to two different characteristics: prosocial behaviors (e.g. kindness) and the ability to successfully achieve social goals (through aggression, if necessary). It isn't necessary to have both characteristics to achieve popularity. Some bullies are simply very good at reaching high status by achieving social goals (such as succeeding in making peers fear and admire them and want to get on their good side). *How* they achieve these goals is viewed differently by different peers. Some see their goal-achieving aggression as effective and even admirable, while others may view the very same behaviors as cruel and self-centered. This helps explain why some bullies are popular and socially successful, and why they may have many friends or admirers, even if they are sometimes cruel.

All this can feel very unfair to the innocent target of a popular bully. And it *is* unfair. But even popular bullies can have other kinds of disadvantages. For example, during one research study conducted five years ago, I showed a peer-conflict scenario to teenagers, and an interesting pattern emerged. Bullies were significantly less likely to notice and identify bullying when it was happening. That cognitive tendency – to misinterpret social information – has been noted in aggressive people before, and in the long run, it can seriously harm a person's life and relationships. How well would someone do in their career if they were constantly being reprimanded for bullying co-workers but completely unable to see the error in their ways? How satisfying would life's relationships be if cruelly dominating a loved one were misperceived as simply a normal relationship? It's important to note that not all bullies showed this cognitive tendency. Overall, bullies were more likely to fail to identify bullying, but most perceived these social situations relatively normally.

It may be comforting to feel superior to your tormenter, but that's not why I'm bringing this up. The fact is, there is no clear and absolute trajectory between childhood bullying and poor or positive life outcomes. Some bullies thrive in life; others don't. Whether a bully or a target does well seems to have more to do with the attention, care, and support they receive while growing up (which is true for almost all youth). As a group, bullies seem to be more likely to encounter problems as they grow up and later in life; but bad outcomes are never a certainty, and some youth who have social problems with peers do "outgrow" them.

To-Do for Myth #12: Bullies have emotional problems.

Most adults who assure kids that a bully has emotional problems are doing so because they hope it will comfort a target. Research suggests, though, that targets of bullying take comfort from these ideas most when other peers also begin to believe them. That is, it may help a little for a parent to focus on a bully's shortcomings; but it helps a lot more if peers can be supportive in how they like a target and how worthwhile they find the target as a friend.

Does this mean that focusing on a bully's problems isn't worth discussing with your child if they are a target? Sometimes it does help a child to consider how troubled or sad a bully might be. At other times, this can feel like cold comfort. Understand that a bully's shortcomings aren't always a helpful concept in the short term, when a child is being actively targeted; in those cases, it's usually better to focus primarily on immediate strategies for feeling better in school or online, including gathering support from friends and school adults, focusing energy and attention on positive activities and skills, and bolstering family time and support. In the long term, though, it may help a former target who's looking back on and reflecting about a bullying episode to understand that aggression never comes from a good place.

Chapter 14
Myth #13
All children all equally vulnerable to bullying.

Are you a 24-hour-news-cycle junkie? Constant information is very stimulating, but you might be surprised to learn that there's uncertainty about the ability of the human brain to correctly interpret so much mass media. For almost all of human existence, the world didn't have social media, the Internet, or even telephones. Very, very recently, newspapers began to be published regularly, but compared to the flow of media information today, they disgorged information much less frequently: for much of the twentieth century, unless you were a city dweller, by the time you saw a newspaper (if at all) it was weeks or months old. How likely were you to hear about rare events? The sheer amount of news that anyone saw a hundred years ago was so much smaller than today's tsunami of contemporary information that people generally learned

25 Myths About Bullying and Cyberbullying, First Edition.
Elizabeth K. Englander.
© 2020 John Wiley & Sons, Inc. Published 2020 by John Wiley & Sons, Inc.

only about the most important stories – war, politics, famine, etc. You might run across a story about someone winning a prize a handful of times in your life. Based on that low frequency, your brain would correctly estimate that prize-winning is unlikely to happen often to anybody. "Do I hear about it regularly?" your brain asks itself. If the answer is "no," your brain sensibly concludes that the odds of such an event occurring are low.

Our brains still ask that question; but today, in the onslaught of media that characterizes the First World, we hear about uncommon events much more often. Consider the lottery. Have you ever won it? The odds of winning any state lottery in the United States are smaller than the odds of having identical quadruplets or being crushed to death by a vending machine[1]; yet you can probably recall many, many times when you've come across news reports of lottery winners. We've all seen photos of smiling winners holding up giant checks. Lottery drawings take place several times a week in some states, with big news stories about each winner. No matter how low the odds of *actually* winning, the regularity of these reports causes your brain to ponder, "How can winning the lottery be so rare, if there are regular reports of lottery winners littering the landscape all around me?"

My point, which I'm now finally getting around to, is that the way your brain interprets frequency data can make you overestimate the odds of an outcome. If you're besieged by media reports about an event, it will come to seem pretty common, even if it's relatively rare. This can considerably increase our anxiety about bullying and the negative outcomes that can happen to targets. In a rational sense, we all know that bullying and cyberbullying hurt some more than others, but how our brains interpret the odds of serious injury are impacted by all the news stories we read about bullying and cyberbullying.

A cursory glance at media and even at scientific media suggests that dire outcomes following bullying are trumpeted from the rooftops. Newspaper stories grimly report on depression, violence, suicides, and homicides following bullying. The titles of the research reports in *LiveScience* are equally unambiguous: "The Pain of

Bullying Lasts Into Adulthood." "Bullying May Leave Worse Mental Scars than Child Abuse." "Teen Bullying Doubles the Adult Risk of Depression." Is it any wonder that a survey conducted in the fall of 2015 by the Pew Research Center found that parents' top concern was that their child would be bullied? That survey found that 60% of parents worried about bullying.[2] Bullying was the most common fear, ahead of anxiety and depression; their child being kidnapped, beaten up, or shot; pregnancy; drugs and alcohol; and their child getting in trouble with the law.

The bad news is that bullying is a real problem, not an imaginary one. But the better news is that it doesn't impact all children in the same way, and truly terrible outcomes are rare. Teenagers I studied in 2015 who were targeted by a bully weren't all affected equally. Resiliency wasn't rare; in fact, almost half (46%) said the bullying or cyberbullying bothered or upset them only a little, or not at all. Almost a third (30%) said it bothered and upset them a great deal, and the final 24% said it impacted them "moderately." Other research has found similar patterns. Some kids are resilient when a bully tries to target them; others are deeply affected. Girls were significantly more impacted than boys; we know that being bullied by a friend is worse than being bullied by an acquaintance, and girls are much more likely to report that their bully is, or was, a friend of theirs. We also know that teens are less impacted as they grow up. In my research, 44% of kids who were bullied in high school reported that the bullying bothered them less and less as time went on; in contrast, only 15% said it bothered them more and more. Most kids cope with bullying, sometimes unhappily, sometimes with true indifference. Some are truly able to cope well and thrive despite others targeting them; their resiliency reminds us how important it is to focus on ways we can help kids foster coping skills. See this chapter's "To-Do List" for some ways we can teach children resiliency.

So while it may seem as though bullying and cyberbullying inevitably result in very serious outcomes, the truth is more complicated. Some kids can cope well; they are resilient. Others are more vulnerable. The same child can be vulnerable at one point during their development, and resilient at another point. In a study of children I conducted in 2018, I compared their resiliency at different ages. Of the children who described themselves as less resilient early in life, 18% developed resiliency by high school. Of the children who described themselves as more resilient in early life, 26% became more vulnerable as they grew. Changeability may not be the norm for a majority of children, but these percentages suggest that for a large minority of children, resiliency can change as you grow up. The trick may be to learn more about what makes people more resilient or more vulnerable and to use that knowledge to help children and teens cope if bullying happens to them.

To-Do for Myth #13: All children all equally vulnerable to bullying.

There are ways to help kids feel stronger and more resilient. A study I conducted in 2013 revealed clues about why some kids are more resilient than others. The most powerful strategy for resiliency is having friends or peers who are willing to stick by you in tough times. When I asked kids which strategies adults suggested, they reported being told to "ignore the bully," or simply to "decide the bully has no power over you." But when I asked what strategies they actually used that *worked*, sticking close to friends was ranked, by far, as the best way to cope when other peers are mean. Not all kids have friends at school; sometimes the most helpful thing we can do to increase resiliency is to provide kids with alternative places to make friends (camp, after-school programs, religious settings, etc.).

We also know that several factors can reduce resiliency. Kids who fight a lot with their friends are, on the whole, less resilient; therefore, helping children learn conflict-resolution skills like negotiation, waiting until you're less upset to take

(*continued*)

action, and getting help from other friends may promote resiliency. Teaching kids to keep conflicts off the Internet and away from digital devices can also promote resiliency; I often see digital communications increase conflict and bullying. Finally, sometimes it can help to understand the need to take extra care when you're already feeling vulnerable. In my research, youngsters who are already dealing with other problems, like depression or family troubles, are far less resilient when it comes to fighting and bullying.

Any tactic that increases social support and improves relationships also increases resiliency, and this is true for family life as well as for socializing with friends. It's easy to forget how much family time means for older children, but time spent playing and enjoying the family together can go far in helping kids feel able to cope when a peer is cruel. It also encourages discussion and reporting to adults at a time when those conversations can mean the most.

Notes

1. Carter, A. (2012). 15 things more likely to happen than winning mega millions. The Daily Beast. http://www.thedailybeast.com/articles/2012/03/30/15-things-more-likely-to-happen-than-winning-mega-millions.html.

2. Pew Research Center. (2015). Six-in-ten parents worry their children might be bullied at some point. http://www.pewsocialtrends.org/2015/12/17/parenting-in-america/st_2015-12-17_parenting-41.

Chapter 15

Myth #14
Bullies are raised in dysfunctional families by parents who are bullies themselves.

Peter and Nancy Lanza were educated and involved parents, by all accounts. Their son Adam, raised in a comfortable middle-class Connecticut town with good schools, clearly had challenges. Adam showed significant social, psychological, and learning difficulties, but his parents sought a lot of help for him. He had treatment from doctors and therapists, as well as academic assistance. Growing up at the same time in California, Elliot Rodger was another upper-middle-class boy who, like Adam, had social problems and whose parents worried about him. Like Adam's parents, Elliot's parents didn't just dismiss his problems; they engaged doctors and therapists to help their son, and it was Elliot's mother

25 Myths About Bullying and Cyberbullying, First Edition.
Elizabeth K. Englander.
© 2020 John Wiley & Sons, Inc. Published 2020 by John Wiley & Sons, Inc.

who called the police when she read about his violent intentions on social media.

Neither of these boys had indifferent or violent parents. In both cases, the parents had resources and education, saw and recognized the troubles their sons were having, and tried to get them professional help and support. Yet both boys did the unthinkable: they committed mass murder. Elliot Rodger gunned down six people at the University of California. Adam Lanza murdered 20 young children and 6 adults at Sandy Hook Elementary School. Both boys committed suicide in the final moments of their crime sprees. Neither boy seemed especially similar to either of his educated and accomplished parents.

When we think of people who commit murder, we generally expect them to come from terrible family lives. And indeed, it's not difficult to find other killers who seem to emerge from murderous parents. Jay Nordlinger, author of "Children of Monsters: An Inquiry into the Sons and Daughters of Dictators," points out that many – but not all – children of notoriously lethal dictators become violent themselves.[1] While we know that parents who are violent are more likely to produce violent children, that is very clearly not always the case. Svetlana, daughter of the most lethal dictator of all time (Josef Stalin), was a troubled but nonviolent person. The point is that on a case-by-case level, predicting which bullying children come from bullying or non-bullying parents can be very difficult.

Still, systematic research on hundreds of teens or children can find general patterns. I decided to test in the lab the proposition that aggressive parents produce aggressive children. In a 2016 study I made of 410 older teens, I had the subjects describe their own aggressive behaviors with peers (if any). Depending on how they answered a series of questions about these aggressive behaviors, I separated them into students who bullied others and those who didn't. Next, I also had them report whether their parents engaged in any type of family violence. Not too surprisingly, families with violence produced more than three times the number of bullies. In those families, more than 20% of teens reported being bullies; whereas in nonviolent families, only 6% reported being bullies.

The effect was even stronger for cyberbullies; 29% of teens from a violent family admitted to cyberbullying peers, versus 7% of those from nonviolent homes.

I was also interested to see if the *style* of parenting (apart from violence) was related to bullying behaviors, so I had the kids rate their parents on a series of personality qualities. Based on those ratings, I separated parents into four groups: *authoritarian* (very strict, and not very loving); *authoritative* (strict but also very loving); *permissive* (not strict at all, but loving); and *indifferent* (neither strict nor loving). The first interesting thing I noted was that while mothers' parenting style did impact whether a child reported becoming a victim, it was *fathers'* parenting style that had the most impact on whether a child became a bully. Twenty-seven percent of the students who reported having an authoritarian father (strict and not loving) were bullies; the numbers in the other three groups (authoritative, permissive, and indifferent) were all much lower, around 11–13%. Fifteen percent of the kids with authoritarian fathers admitted to being cyberbullies, while 6–8% of the other parents produced cyberbullies. While we may think of mothers as having much more influence with children, there was no similar pattern for the mothers in this study.

These findings do seem to bear out the idea that bullying kids may come from parents who are violent, or are too strict and not affectionate enough – but, as usual, I'm going to point out that it often isn't that simple. Having a violent or rigid, unaffectionate father might increase the chance that you'll become a bully, but it's not a simple, direct cause. Fully 80% of the bullies came from non-violent families, and more than 70% of the bullies came from families without authoritarian fathers. Looked at from the other direction, about 65% of the kids who came from a violent family did *not* become bullies. But while these numbers seem to negate the whole relationship, you can see the influence of violent families when you examine the kids who didn't become bullies. Consider this: it may be true that 65% of kids from a violent family didn't bully, but fully 87% from a nonviolent family didn't bully. Having a violent family increased the chances of becoming a bully by 12% – not a monumental increase, but a statistically significant one.[2]

Taken together, both the data and individual cases suggest that violent parents do contribute to the violence of their children – at least partly. So maybe our myth isn't entirely a myth. But assuming that the parents of bullies must invariably be bullies themselves is clearly unwarranted. The statistical relationship won't help us predict anything on a case-by-case basis. Instead, it helps us understand social factors that increase the odds of bullying behaviors.

To-Do for Myth #14: Bullies are raised in dysfunctional families by parents who are bullies themselves.

The real danger with this myth is that parents may believe that if they themselves are not bullies, then there is little to no chance that their child will be a bully. But cases and data all point to a different conclusion. Being a violent or rigid, unaffectionate parent does increase the odds that your child will bully others; but even parents who care and do their best by their children can sometimes, despite their best efforts and intentions, raise aggressive kids.

As with so many other parenting factors, the real to-do here is to keep the communication going. Make sure you know what your kids are up to socially, and ask them how they're feeling about their friends and their place in school and online. If another adult (e.g. someone at school, or another parent) complains that your child is a bully, try not to be defensive. Listening respectfully and considering what they say doesn't mean you must ultimately agree. Keep in mind that it's always possible to partially agree and to use that information to start a conversation with your child about how others can sometimes view their behaviors differently than they intend.

Notes

1. Nordlinger, J. (2015). Children of Monsters: An Inquiry Into the Sons and Daughters of Dictators, New York: Encounter Books.
2. I'm using the term *statistically significant* here as researchers use it, to mean that the difference is extremely unlikely to just be a chance finding. We're 95% sure it's a real difference, although it may not be a large difference.

Chapter 16
Myth #15
Revenge is an effective way to handle bullies.

Where were you on January 28, 1986? Even if you don't remember your activities on that date, I'd bet you remember the day when the Challenger shuttle exploded shortly after takeoff. That explosion was one of those national tragedies that people tend to remember vividly. What's less well known, but equally incredible, is that only the day before the takeoff, Bob Ebeling and four other engineers at NASA tried to delay the launch. They were convinced that the shuttle was going to blow up. And blow up it did, taking the lives of all the astronauts on board. Thirty years later, in an NPR interview, Ebeling described how the NASA administration simply didn't want to hear the truth. They just wanted the mission to go forward.

This type of willful denial might not seem terribly relevant to bullying and cyberbullying. Generally speaking, there aren't multiple lives at risk when it comes to most incidents. But consider this:

25 Myths About Bullying and Cyberbullying, First Edition.
Elizabeth K. Englander.
© 2020 John Wiley & Sons, Inc. Published 2020 by John Wiley & Sons, Inc.

sometimes we see people behaving in a way that invites future disaster, and we *just don't want to think about it*. It's even harder when you see a behavior that could cause problems later but that seems to be working, at least for now. Sometimes, the strategies that kids use to deal with bullying can turn around and cause them serious problems later; but we may not want to see the truth in that.

Take the issue of revenge. Decades ago, when tolerance of physical violence in children was much greater, targets were routinely advised to take revenge by hitting a bully back. Today, that strategy is generally a nonstarter. For one thing, most bullying isn't physical any longer. But even when it is, hitting back isn't tolerated, and a bully may turn around and report the target to adults. Whether or not targets genuinely believe they are sticking up for themselves, they may instead reap a punishment, regardless of who was a victim first. Most adults today know to take context into account, but aggression is generally still not tolerated. Bullies today may know how to work the system to their own advantage, and provoking a target into hitting them can strengthen their power instead of diminishing it.

But there are non-physical forms of revenge (like spreading rumors online, or name-calling) that might conceivably work, at least temporarily. It's not pleasant to think of our kids being mean back, but denying that it ever happens is willful blindness. In a 2016 Massachusetts Aggression Reduction Center (*MARC*) study, 32% of the teens who were targets of bullying said that revenge worked for them, at least partially. But it's important to remember that even if antisocial strategies sometimes work, adults shouldn't recommend them. And that's not because we want to deprive kids of a strategy that could be effective; it's because antisocial strategies (i) are much less effective today; (ii) can backfire; and (iii) don't help kids learn the long-term coping skills that will really serve them in the long run.

It's also true that predicting how a bully will respond to revenge is tricky. In the case of physical bullying, it's not hard to see how a bully might shrink from a physical beating, especially if it's public and humiliating. But digital or verbal comebacks can feel much more winnable. For example, a bully who is angry about a revenge attempt could simply construct an anonymous identity and bring down a volley of online attacks on a target's head. Doing this doesn't risk physical safety or public shaming. The revenge that was intended to stop the bullying could end up escalating it.

A fairly recent twist on this problem is when parents undertake digital revenge in the defense of their child, who they feel is being unfairly targeted online. In the field, I increasingly run into school administrators who are dealing with situations in which parents take revenge into their own hands: for example, by texting back a bully using their child's phone (and not always with their child's consent). Doing this is understandable because it's so distressing to see your child being put down online; but it often escalates a problem situation and makes things worse for your child. There's little research on this, but cyberbullies don't seem to be as reliably cowed by a target using digital technology to "hit back" as physical bullies are presumed to be by literally being hit back. And that suggests that digital revenge (whether it's done by the target or the target's parents) is less likely to stop a cyberbullying situation. It may, in fact, escalate the situation dramatically and make things worse for your child. But while that outcome is unsure, one thing is pretty certain to happen if you personally fire off mean messages to your child's cyberbully: you're sending a clear message to your child. You are taking action because you don't believe that your child – even with support and coaching – can handle themselves socially. And that lack of faith is likely to have a real impact on your son or daughter.

Dealing with difficult and mean people is an incredibly helpful life skill that can be, and typically is, learned while you're young. There's a slim chance that a contemporary teenager would get away with punching a bully, but even if they did, that's not exactly a life lesson. Anybody is much less likely to get away with it as an adult, when the full force of the law could result in an assault charge. Hitting back is what I call a *high-risk, low-return* strategy. It's really difficult to do, and it's also likely to fail. In contrast, let's focus on *low-risk, high-return* strategies: tactics that are easier to do and more likely to result in resilience and positive outcomes.

The good news is that there definitely are such strategies. When we've asked targets of bullying what actually helps, one strategy emerges as the most successful: learning how to garner support and help from friends and family. It's potent to realize the power of sticking close to your friends, confiding in them and getting advice, and talking with peers and family about what's happening to you. This is true for a couple of reasons. First, talking about a problem can reduce its power. Just speaking aloud about your strong emotions with someone you trust can make bring some emotional relief. But talking with people who love them can also remind vulnerable victims that they're not alone and they're not worthless, no matter what a bully says to them. This type of strategy is what I call *low risk, high return* for a few reasons. It's something that every adult can recommend. It's also a strategy that kids can easily learn and keep using their entire life. Mean people will always exist; but our ability to be strong and resilient in the face of their cruelty can be greatly enhanced by social support.

To-Do for Myth #15: Revenge is an effective way to handle bullies.

Kids with a ready set of supportive friends are the lucky ones. But what if your child has few or even no friends at school?

There's no magic answer to this dilemma. But if your child is struggling to learn to make friends, you should focus on that issue. Sometimes kids who struggle to make friends in school do better in other settings. For example, a child who feels isolated at school might be able to make friends at camp, or during an after-school activity. Friendships are also easier to pursue during shared interests: think about sports, music, art, or other activities your child enjoys, and pursue those interests in social settings. Although it's always helpful to have friends at school, sometimes making friends outside of school helps to develop social skills enough to

(*continued*)

help a child begin to form friendships in school. And even if your child can't, or doesn't, ever make friends at school, having social support outside of school definitely helps.

And don't forget the power of family. If your child has siblings who are willing or able, ask them to stick close. They don't need to publicly defend their sibling (although it's nice if they feel up to that); just being there (and not ignoring their sister or brother) can help.

Finally, adult support isn't the same as peers, but it still helps. Your support for your child is crucial, and there are likely sympathetic adults at your child's school as well. Think about the teachers your son or daughter likes, the school counselors, the administrators, even the school nurse. A sympathetic ear – even a grownup one – is a lot better than feeling isolated when someone's being mean to you.

Chapter 17
Myth #16
Bullies don't understand how much they're hurting the target.

Never argue with a six-year-old who shaves.

– Calvin and Hobbes

Perhaps you remember Moe, the beefy, iconic bully in the Calvin and Hobbes comic strip. "Are your maladjusted antisocial tendencies the product of your berserk pituitary gland?" Calvin asks Moe, who pauses for a lengthy period of time before asking, "What?"

Bullies have changed a lot since this stereotype, which depicted bullying as primarily physical and bullies as kids who tended to be physically large and have poor academic performance and low social status. Other kids might have been afraid of them, but they didn't want to *be* them. When stereotypical physical bullying

25 Myths About Bullying and Cyberbullying, First Edition.
Elizabeth K. Englander.
© 2020 John Wiley & Sons, Inc. Published 2020 by John Wiley & Sons, Inc.

happened, no one questioned if bullies knew they were hurting their victims. They were the ones throwing the punches – so of course they knew.

But once adults, and society in general, grew much less tolerant of childish aggression, bullies started to use psychological tactics more frequently – verbal, relational, and (eventually) digital attacks, to be exact. And that change in tactics raised the possibility that bullying could conceivably, at times, be inadvertent. If you threw a punch, you clearly meant to hurt someone. But if you throw a mean comment, it can, maybe, be the result of thoughtlessness or clumsy phrasing.

You may remember that bullying is about ongoing, repetitive, deliberate attacks. *By definition*, bullying happens on purpose. But there are many other kinds of conflicts between kids where social cruelty can be accidental. For example, it's not hard to imagine how unintentional cruelty could happen between very young children or kids with significantly delayed social skills. And it goes without saying that even older, more typical kids can (and do) make mistakes. A kid might say something mean once, carelessly, without thinking, even to a friend (or sometimes *especially* to a friend). They can fight with or try to provoke peers. They can be in a cranky mood and snap at someone at school or online. Cruelty between kids can be accidental or purposeful, but it can also be somewhere in between – incidents can be deliberate, but more hurtful (or taken further) than the aggressor intended. And I'll ironically point out what we all know – that children can be thoughtless at times, acting and speaking without thinking.

There's no doubt that most kids have incidents where they genuinely don't realize they're being hurtful. In a 2016 research study, I asked teens to reflect on their socially mean behaviors toward their peers. About 38% said that during one incident or another, they didn't realize how cruelly they were behaving.[1]

Even more common is when a teen admits to being temporarily *unwilling* to be empathic. Sometimes kids are aware of the hurt they're causing, but they'd rather not think about how it feels to be on the receiving end. They'd rather focus, instead, on their own feelings. For example, they may retaliate against a mean remark in the school cafeteria by throwing back their own verbal barb. They're a little mad, perhaps, and they know that what they're saying is mean, but they're not focusing on the target's feelings – instead, they're focusing on other kids seeing them get the upper hand socially. Almost 73% of the kids who were mean to a peer fell into this category at least some of the time. They agreed with statements like, "The way I acted wasn't ideal, but it was understandable." In these situations, kids minimize their bad behaviors and avoid lingering on how much hurt they're causing. They often justify their actions. These are the situations where kids tend to benefit most from being persuaded to face how hurtful they've been.

Finally, there is a third type of incident where the aggressor completely and utterly lacks empathy. While this type of bully might appear similar to other types on the outside, such a bully has absolutely no internal struggle and no reservations about what they're doing. They don't excuse their behavior by seeing it as bad but understandable for some reason. These types of kids may believe that they're entirely justified in what they do, that they're only behaving in a way that's just and reasonable, and that it's fun to see someone else squirm. I think this is the most upsetting type of bullying, but it's also the least common, luckily. In my experience, these bullies are unusual; only 18% of the kids who were mean described incidents where they felt this way. During these incidents, a bully knows perfectly well that they're hurting someone, yet they completely lack compassion for the target's suffering – they revel in the target's hurt. What's tricky is that it's difficult to tell this type of bully apart from the others, because even when bullies question their own behavior, they may appear callous and indifferent on the outside.

But when we ask whether a bully knows that they're hurting the target, in a way we're missing an important issue. Bullying doesn't just affect targets, after all; it impacts the entire climate in a school. What I mean is that social cruelty and bullying can make a school feel like a hostile and unwelcoming place for many children. Bullies often focus on the impact they're having on a target, but what they don't often appreciate is the impact they're having on their entire school atmosphere. In fact, the larger harm of bullying is the impact on all the kids who attend a school, in a sense. Yet children who are socially aggressive often miss this point.

Bottom line: do bullies always know they're hurting others? Most repetitive incidents *are* intentional, but there are some exceptions (like kids who may not read social signals accurately). But it's also important to remember that most social cruelty between kids isn't bullying per se, and it can sometimes be chalked up to carelessness, thoughtlessness, temporary anger, or (also often temporary) willful disregard for the feelings of the target. There are kids who are truly cruel to others and enjoy their target's agony, but these children are the exception – not the rule.

To-Do for Myth #16: Bullies don't understand how much they're hurting the target.

In a way, our laser-like focus on bullying has limited the flexibility of our responses to social cruelty in general. We've identified bullying as the problem – and in so doing we may be ignoring fighting or the milder types of social cruelty that can sometimes lead to bullying.

If we want to reduce bullying, adults need to respond to all types of inappropriate social conflicts. Letting kids know our expectations is a difficult but short-lived challenge. It's difficult because setting expectations means consistently responding to inappropriate social behaviors. For example, if your child calls a sibling a name, it's tempting to just let it slide – and occasionally that might be fine. But it's better to let your child know that name-calling is not OK – not with anyone; not ever. By calling out those milder behaviors, you'll be helping to prevent the ascent into more serious behavioral problems.

(*continued*)

You can also promote compassion by making sure you recognize, call out, and praise kind acts – and by modeling them yourselves. All of this sounds easier than it is, in our fast-paced world, where so many different things tug at our attention. But start by just becoming more aware of kindness and how important it is. Fred Rogers ("Mr. Rogers' Neighborhood") often described how, during a tragedy, his mother would point out the helpers to him, instead of emphasizing the suffering:

> When I was a boy and I would see scary things in the news, my mother would say to me, "Look for the helpers. You will always find people who are helping."

Pointing out kind acts has the added benefit of helping your child understand how much goodness and helpfulness there is in the world – and isn't that a world view we all want our children to share?

Note

1. As you keep reading, you'll notice that the percentages don't add up to 100%. That's because some teens reported different types of empathy and compassion in different situations.

Chapter 18
Myth #17
Schools don't do anything about bullying.

When a young person commits suicide, it's a failure for all of society. Suicide by adults is appalling and tragic enough; but when a child or teenager takes their own life, it exposes how the adults in our society have failed to nurture and protect them. The pain for their parents is almost unimaginable.

Bullying may be a contributing factor, in some cases, to suicide in youth. In 2016, Daniel Fitzpatrick, a student in a private school in New York, hanged himself. The news media and his heartbroken father blamed the boy's school. Lesser such incidents occur every day in this country, and I often get emails from parents who are frustrated by what they perceive as a lack of response from their child's school to a bullying situation. But is it true that schools just don't care about bullying?

There are two important points here. First, while no profession boasts 100% perfection, I think very few educators are genuinely

25 Myths About Bullying and Cyberbullying, First Edition.
Elizabeth K. Englander.
© 2020 John Wiley & Sons, Inc. Published 2020 by John Wiley & Sons, Inc.

indifferent to suffering in their students. Until relatively recently, though, it is true that many teachers, administrators, *and* parents felt that bullying was a comparatively normal rite of passage and not likely to do any serious harm. In my experience – and I work with dozens of schools every year – those attitudes among adults are far less common than they used to be. Ten to 15 years ago, I regularly met educators who simply didn't buy the idea that bullying was a problem at *their* school. Even in the face of tragic consequences associated with a bullying situation, that denial sometimes persisted. About a decade ago, I worked in a school where a bullied girl had committed suicide, and she had told others that she felt there was no adult at school she could talk to. "I just don't believe it," the principal said. "There's no bullying here; any kid here can talk to anybody." In the face of what had just happened to this school community, I found his denial astonishing. Today, though, I see a dramatic increase in interest and concern about bullying and cyberbullying; most educators are much more aware of the scope and depth of these problems, and everyone has seen the public shaming that schools go through when a bullied child commits suicide or a violent act.

Apart from the idea that schools don't care about bullying, I think there are a few factors that unfortunately but persistently contribute to the (often mistaken) impression that schools sweep bullying under the rug – even when they don't.

First, adults are less likely to react to bullying that happens right in front of them – not because they don't care, but because bullying behaviors are subtler and thus harder to recognize today. When kids today are cranky, mad at someone, or bullying someone, they're all equally likely to use indirect acts or words of contempt (these are called *gateway behaviors*) as a way of hurting the other person. Examples of gateway behaviors might be rolling your eyes when someone says something; ignoring someone who's speaking, as though they're invisible; excluding or laughing at someone; or name-calling. Think of gateway behaviors as though they were a skin rash. If you have Lyme disease, you get a rash. But not every rash means you have Lyme disease. Lyme disease is only one possible cause of a rash; there are many other possible causes. Likewise, bullies use gateway behaviors, but gateway behaviors don't always mean bullying is going on. Gateway behaviors happen all the time; they're used when kids are mad at each other, when they're bullying each other, or when they're just annoyed or thoughtless. Gateway behaviors are not invisible; adults see kids using them, but because they are minor transgressions, the motive behind them is usually presumed to be similarly minor in importance. Unless teachers are specifically trained otherwise, they may not realize that gateway behaviors can indicate bullying is happening. When you see eye-rolling constantly, it's easy to assume that it's not a big deal, and adults often assume that bullying will be much more dramatic and obvious.

To illustrate this, imagine a classroom where one student gets an answer wrong, and two others titter and laugh, which makes the target feel stupid. The teacher sees and hears the laughter, but he has no way of knowing what's going on; he may assume the kids are being thoughtless, or showing off for friends, or even possibly mad at the target. He doesn't realize that the two laughers have been picking on the target for quite a while. But even if the teacher doesn't know what is happening, the kids typically know the backstory. They know this isn't a random gesture and that it's part of a bullying campaign against the target that's been going on since the third grade. Being made fun of when you get an answer wrong is always unpleasant, but if you're chronically being bullied, it can be truly wounding. So, the target goes home and tells her parents that bullying happened *right in front of the teacher*, but the teacher did nothing in response. The teacher's take is that all he saw was some mean giggling; he may be wrong, but he's not deliberately lying or covering up anything; and if the parent complains, the teacher may view the complaint as a categorical overreaction.

It's exactly this sort of situation that I try to rectify by training educators about what gateway behaviors are and how to respond to them. Teachers don't necessarily see "bullying" per se; what they see are gateway behaviors, which may or may not indicate bullying. Rather than attempting to guess if bullying's going on, educators should recognize that gateway behaviors are hurtful and always socially inappropriate. In one training session I ran with a group of teachers, I had them practice responding to these small acts of contempt. One middle school teacher commented, "I can't believe, now, that I always just let this stuff go." Learning how impactful an accumulation of supposedly minor gateway behaviors can be is eye-opening.

The second reason that schools may appear indifferent has to do with our expectations about privacy and confidentiality. Educators are trained to keep all behavior problems and their consequences confidential. They're not stonewalling your desire for information; they're obeying a law they've been trained on meticulously. But when a victim or their parents want to know what the consequences will be for a bully, it's hard to be told "That's confidential." That response feels as though the bully is being unduly protected. Schools need to do a better job of communicating with victims and parents about the limits that are placed on them by law, reassuring them that the problem is not being ignored or forgotten, and taking steps to make the child feel safer. These things can absolutely be accomplished without violating confidentiality laws.

The third reason that schools may appear deceptively indifferent to bullying is the overuse of the term. The word *bullying* gets everyone's blood pressure up, and if our child is struggling socially, we want the school to care. But using the word when kids are fighting, or when a child is hypersensitive, can backfire. When we fail to recognize that a problem is actually a two-way fight, or that a child may be perceiving bullying when it's not happening (which is much more common than most parents think), we contribute to "label fatigue." We make it more likely that educators will be exhausted by, and less responsive to, continual claims of bullying.

Finally, as a parent myself, I'd like to think that my child's school could simply fix bullying when it happens. But when they fail to do that, it's not always because they're not trying. If a bully is targeting a victim through words and looks, it's difficult to see how any school could control that. The children involved will see each other in school, even if they're kept largely apart; they'll pass each other in the hallway, or see each other in the lunchroom or on the bus. A bully can obey an edict to not speak to or look at a target, and still succeed in making them feel small. Comments through other students, laughter in class and the lunchroom, pointed exclusion – these are all common but don't violate "no-contact" rules. In other words, it's hard to hear, but I do think parents need to accept the reality that in *some* circumstances, adults cannot completely stop bullying. I truly wish it weren't so, but this is why I always emphasize the importance of supporting kids and helping them be resilient. Schools and adults may not be able to entirely stop a bully who gets their friends to go after their target, or bullies online where adults won't see; but they can, and should, always support a child who's a target so that they don't feel alone, abandoned, unloved by family, and disliked by adults and peers. And because that is an approach that can always be used and is always helpful, there's never an excuse for not doing your utmost to support a child.

To-Do for Myth #17: Schools don't do anything about bullying.

Educators need to explain confidentiality law to parents, and they need to do so in a skilled and detailed manner to minimize any misunderstandings about why they're not offering more information about a particular case or the handling of a case. The Massachusetts Aggression Reduction Center has a free download that can help educators and parents understand confidentiality: https://www.englanderelizabeth.com/downloads.

Educators also need to emphasize to parents that whether or not a case is designated as *bullying* isn't the most

(continued)

(*continued*)
important thing; what's most important are the actions that are taken to resolve and improve a situation. Those actions need to be the focus.

For their part, parents need to consider practicality; are there practical measures that can be taken to help a child feel better and safer in school? Bodyguards and instant expulsion of accused bullies typically are not realistic options. Don't only focus on punishment; focus on positive actions that can help a target feel safer and better, like increasing opportunities for them to be near friends, expanding their social opportunities so that they can make new and different friends, having a "safe adult" in school, and checking in with both parents and the victim regularly.

Chapter 19

Myth #18

Schools can't take any action in cyberbullying cases.

W hen my children were going through middle school, they all pestered me for cell phones. They wanted one. Their friends had cell phones. In fact, they were the only 11-year-olds on the planet without one! I generally resisted (which was easier 10 years ago), but I ended up buying my third child a "dumb phone" – a phone that only lets you make phone calls. He found this experience to be an exercise in learned helplessness: that is, learning to accept defeat when there's nothing you can do about a situation. One morning, as he headed out the door, I noticed he had left his cell phone on the kitchen counter. When I pointed this out to him, instead of taking it with him to school, he despaired: "Why should I take it? It doesn't *do* anything." Apparently, making phone calls with a cell phone doesn't actually count as a function.

25 Myths About Bullying and Cyberbullying, First Edition.
Elizabeth K. Englander.
© 2020 John Wiley & Sons, Inc. Published 2020 by John Wiley & Sons, Inc.

Learned helplessness can afflict schools, too, especially when it comes to digital technology. Much if not most social media and Internet use, after all, takes place off campus, or doesn't use campus equipment, thus limiting the jurisdiction a school has over digital types of misbehavior. Texas passed a law in 2017 that permits schools to discipline students based on their out-of-school social media posts, but schools in most states don't have such control.[1] Still, while schools typically have little of the authority, they suffer a lot of the consequences and have retained a lot of the responsibility for education about digital technology. Today, schools are expected to teach kids about how to use digital devices. They've also become the purveyors of education about social skills and emotional functioning. Schools have to deal with the decrease in attention and the increase in anxiety and depression that can be linked with technology and social media use. They may have to battle students *and* parents when technology rules are laid down. And parents often go directly to the school when cyberbullying occurs.

That's where the dilemma begins. Schools are generally viewed as more knowledgeable about cyberbullying and social media problems; and they clearly have jurisdiction over bullying that happens in school. But outside of school, where much if not most digital communication occurs, schools are not in charge – parents are. Thus a school administrator may feel obliged to turn away a parent who needs help with a situation where their child is being targeted on social media, because the administrator may view such situations as beyond their jurisdiction. In a sense, they've been taught to be helpless when it comes to digital forms of bullying.

But educators aren't as helpless as they may feel, and parents may need to help their child's school personnel understand what they can do to help a target of cyberbullying who's embroiled in this type of situation. It's true that a school's ability to *discipline* an offending child solely for what they do to others online may be limited or even nonexistent, but there are many other actions a school can take to help the child who's being victimized online. For example, schools can monitor the situation and see if the cyberbullying "spills over" into school. As I pointed out in an earlier chapter, what happens in school and what happens online between kids are much less separate than adults tend to believe. Half or more of the incidents reported in MARC's research involve *both* school and digital interactions. In elementary school, problems that happened both online and in school were much, much more common than problems that happened only online. This means if your child is being targeted on social media, there's a very good chance that some problems are happening in school as well – and those are cases where the school has clear jurisdiction and can take action immediately.

In addition, providing support and care helps all kids deal with any type of social problem, including those that occur through digital technology. At home, that can mean listening and talking, and possibly brainstorming about different strategies or approaches. In school, any child can be assigned a "safe person" – an adult, like an assistant principal or the school nurse – who they have permission to go see whenever they feel uncomfortable or want to talk. (In my experience, most children who have a safe person don't go to see them often; but simply having them available can be very reassuring and comforting.)

Finally, prevention is always better than a cure. Schools can work to address these problems and improve the school environment. They can utilize class discussions, as well as social and emotional curricula and lesson plans, to help youngsters discuss, identify, and respond to social cruelty, both in school and in digital environments. They can encourage youth to help targets of cruelty, and they can help kids understand why gateway behaviors are so poisonous.

It's understandable that a parent might feel frustrated because none of these actions involve actually punishing the bully. But few of the subjects I study who are bullied emphasize that punishment is, in their opinion, the best option. In 2018, less than 10% of the targets of bullying I studied believed that punishment for the bully "almost always" helped resolve a bullying situation. More than half felt that punishment might help in some cases but not in others, and 37% felt that punishment rarely helps. Almost all the kids viewed a focus on punishment as at least somewhat misguided. For parents, this suggests that directing too much attention toward punishment may not always be the best way to support your child if they're a target; and the prospect of their parents insisting on a bully's punishment can sometimes even result in kids feeling reluctant to talk to their parents about social problems. It's also helpful to keep in mind that as the parent of the victim, you often will not know about any punishment another child endures (remember: it is legally confidential information), even when that other child is a bully who's been targeting your son or daughter. While social strategies can help a target feel more capable and resilient, punishment may make them feel more fearful that retaliation is forthcoming.

Of course, as a society, we also have to consider how best to help children who bully. Consequences (i.e. punishment) can help them understand where social lines are drawn, and what is and isn't acceptable behavior. But punishment will only take us so far with this problem. Ultimately, children who bully may respond better to help and therapy than to punishment, and consequences need to be more powerful than suspending a child (which is often simply experienced as a vacation). I don't mean to throw out the baby with the bathwater here. Some focus on punishment is completely reasonable and understandable; but when adults focus on reprimands too much, that can discourage targets from approaching them for help. In the long run, building up resiliency and improving the school climate so that other kids don't support bullying can be better strategies.

To-Do for Myth #18: Schools can't take any action in cyberbullying cases.

When your child is being hurt, one of the first emotions you may experience is anger. That anger is usually directed at the child who's being cruel (the "bully" or "aggressor"), and it can be intense. As a result, you may focus solely on your desire to punish that child. But as I pointed out earlier,

(continued)

schools may lack the jurisdiction to punish a student who misbehaves off-campus (that is, online). In addition, punishment of an aggressor isn't always the most desirable thing from your child's point of view. In fact, emotional support is what children consistently rate as most helpful when they're being bullied. With this in mind, it can be more productive to focus on supporting your child and making sure that the school supports them.

With the school, consider your options. A "safe adult" can be assigned to help your child upon request; make sure that adult is someone your child likes and feels they can talk to. You can negotiate the rules for the safe person with the school administration. For example, your child can be given permission to see this adult anytime they feel the need; and a prearranged signal can be arranged with your son or daughter's teacher. Other in-school actions can be helpful, too; consider a prearranged lunch table, where your child can be seated with other friendly kids. Structured play can be offered as an alternative activity on the playground, and it can help targets of bullying avoid aggressors. Seat assignments can help reduce the stress of having to find a "safe seat" on the bus.

Support at home always helps, as well. Being calm, helping your child strategize, and checking in with them can make them feel as though these situations can be coped with; on the other hand, a parent who's demonstrating an intense emotional reaction can be scary and can make a child feel like a situation is out of control. If possible, spend some extra time with your child, and go do something fun. In a busy household, this is something you'll probably need to plan in advance; but it can be well worth the effort, and those private times with you are something your child may always remember.

Note

1. Bogan, R. (2017). Texas anti-cyberbullying law gives schools more enforcement authority. Fox News. https://www.foxnews.com/us/texas-anti-cyberbullying-law-gives-schools-more-enforcement-authority.

Chapter 20
Myth #19
Schools could absolutely stop bullying if they wanted to.

Zero-tolerance policies – policies that compel standardized, one-size-fits-all responses to aggressive behaviors – can seem like a very good idea when it comes to problems like bullying. If you misbehave, you reap the consequences – period. The penalties are predetermined and are applied equally in every case. There's no room for adults to make a judgment call, and you can't have cases where one bully is punished while another bully is let off scot-free. As every parent knows, consistency is key when you want an undesirable behavior to stop.

But while this sounds like a good way to be consistent and clear about not tolerating bullying or cyberbullying, in real life,

25 Myths About Bullying and Cyberbullying, First Edition.
Elizabeth K. Englander.
© 2020 John Wiley & Sons, Inc. Published 2020 by John Wiley & Sons, Inc.

zero-tolerance policies in schools don't work well. The fact is that when it comes to kids, crafting appropriate consequences is more an art than a science, and individual circumstances, situations, and actors need to be taken into account. Zero-tolerance policies don't permit the necessary degree of flexibility; they're so rigid that absurd situations can easily develop; and far from being absurdly funny, these situations can be very damaging to children. Take Samuel Burgos' case in Florida. He brought a gun to school and was promptly expelled, which sounds fine until you realize that Sam was only seven years old, the gun in question was a toy, and he never took it out of his backpack. Despite all this, a zero-tolerance policy in his school dictated his expulsion. In Florida, a young girl found a knife in her lunchbox – placed there by her mother for the purpose of cutting up her apple. She immediately gave the knife to a teacher but was still expelled for bringing a weapon to school. Another draconian consequence was applied to a teenager who was caught in school talking to his mother on his cell phone; she was deployed in the military overseas and he had not spoken to her in a month, but using his phone violated a zero-tolerance policy and he was expelled.

These cases illustrate the problems with zero-tolerance policies. If you don't consider every single possible scenario in advance and bake every possible exception into the rules, the consequences can often make no sense. And if you do try to include every possible allowance (not for kids under 11? not if the gun is a toy? not if your mother is in a war zone?) then the policy can be convoluted, confusing, and possibly ineffective and inconsistent.

Zero-tolerance policies to address bullying were widely applied in almost 80% of schools during the 1990s and 2000s, but they were subsequently abandoned as unworkable and too often discriminatory. A multitude of studies showed that these inflexible consequences, which were touted as a good way to reduce bullying through the equal and mindless application of identical discipline, ended up being clearly disproportionately applied to kids of color,

LGBTQ kids, and ethnic and religious minorities. For example, one typical study of 142 schools in Florida[1] found that black males were suspended at disproportionately higher rates than white males at every school level (elementary, middle, and high school). Overall, 12% of white males were suspended, compared to 26% of black males. In a system that was supposed to indiscriminately apply discipline, black males had more than double the rate of suspensions. Special needs students have also been disciplined under zero-tolerance policies at disproportionate rates; this is especially true for youth who have emotional and behavioral disabilities.[2] But the failure of zero-tolerance policies wasn't only about its discriminatory application – it was also about these policies' inability to improve the school climate and reduce bullying and cyberbullying. A review of the policies notes that zero-tolerance policies can interfere with relationships and trust between kids and adults; that they can exacerbate mental health problems in vulnerable kids; and that their lack of emphasis on prevention and treatment can harm the school climate and increase society's cost burden by increasing the proportion of children who end up on public welfare programs or in prison.[3] Unfortunately, getting rid of zero-tolerance policies has sometimes led to the misconception that schools are simply avoiding a task they could accomplish – namely, entirely getting rid of bullying and cyberbullying. That sense, that feeling, has lingered, and it can be confusing when we're faced with a much more complex reality.

Taking a step back and thinking about what *school* is can help clarify this. School is a place where children interact with each other. Large pockets of time are structured, with more formal interactions, but significant portions of the day are informal. Classrooms are formal, but playgrounds, lunchrooms, school buses, and some classes are less structured and more free-wheeling. At school, children learn about academic subjects, but they also learn about social relationships. School is a challenging place, where kids have to form relationships with people who aren't related to them and don't necessarily know them. There's a rigid and overt power structure among the children that dominates many of their social interactions. Rules are enforced. One of the most important rules is the prohibition against telling everything to adults; any violation of that rule can result in severe social consequences. And while of course there are adults who watch over, care for, and greatly influence the children, there's typically a small adult-to-child ratio. School is a place where children must learn how to interact with peers on their own, hopefully with the support of friends but typically without the constant hovering of adults.

All this means that expecting schools to exert complete and total control over every child's looks, actions, words, and feelings is a losing proposition. Just think about a typical situation from a practical point of view. Picture a boy who's being targeted by a group of peers. They post comments and pictures about him online, or exchange messages. At school, they laugh openly in the hallways when he walks by. Maybe they trip him in a hallway or pull down the books he's holding. In the lunchroom, they look his way and make fun of him. Now, some of these actions might be seen by adults and could easily trigger a consequence or an intervention. If an adult happened to see the target being tripped, or his books being pulled down, or a seat being denied him on the bus, they could do something. But a lot of these behaviors aren't cause for discipline. For example, adults likely have no idea what the boys are doing with social media and messages on their phones. There's no rule against looking or laughing, or talking with friends. Those actions certainly aren't grounds for suspension or expulsion. Realistically, what could a school do?

Actually, there are many actions a school could take to help resolve this situation *apart* from suspension or expulsion. For example, any school could offer the target emotional support; the school could try to keep him near his friends, warn potential bullies, look for harassment, and stop problems when they're seen. Schools can try to hamper bullying by, for example, separating bullies and targets in class, but this isn't logistically always possible. (I've worked in small schools that had only one class per grade.) But they can't take action if they're not told about what is happening, and schools aren't always given complete (or even any) details about the harassment. Actions they do take often can't be instantaneous, because many states and districts have laws and policies that obligate schools to investigate bullying situations, which usually means they cannot immediately believe, and act on, everything a target tells them. Just imagine the repercussions if a school instantly expelled all students accused of bullying. A bully could terrorize potential targets by simply threatening to falsely report them to adults, with the ensuring expulsion doing their work for them.

All this makes it probable that school administrators won't be able to *immediately* stop harassment, although by talking to all parties, taking action, and monitoring the situation, it may end eventually. Still, reality aside, it's completely understandable why any parent (or any target, for that matter) would want bullying to stop the same day it's reported. But addressing bullying and cyberbullying in a school is often a lengthy process, having to do with watching a situation, administering consequences when possible, improving a target's support and resilience by encouraging friendships, and actively working to maintain a positive school climate.

This sounds like bad news, but it isn't always. When targets of bullying are surveyed by researchers, they report that what helps them the most isn't instant punishment or consequences for bullies but rather immediate support, advice, and someone to talk to. Being emotionally supportive may not feel like "taking action," but it's the action that kids rate as most helpful, and it can be started without delay. School personnel might know that they may be criticized for focusing on supporting the target instead of concentrating on the instant punishment of an accused bully. But in the long run, being unable to instantly resolve the situation may not be what's most important; and parents can help schools strategize most effectively when they understand what's both helpful *and* possible.

To-Do for Myth #19: Schools could absolutely stop bullying if they wanted to.

In general, bullying isn't the type of problem that can be instantly resolved, although adults can take immediate actions that can bring fast relief. In some circumstances, bullying can be stopped. If a child is harassing others on the bus, re-seating them near the driver or ultimately taking them off the bus can work. But bullying is often a situation where the bad behavior isn't confined to a specific place or time, and it can be supported by other students. That means that focusing on one area (e.g. the bus) or one person (e.g. the ringleader) won't always be possible or effective.

In the face of bullying, adults want to act. Focusing on support, family, and friendships can be the most fruitful approach in helping children cope successfully. All efforts should still be made to stop a bullying situation, but in my research (and others'), victims report that it's the efforts of others to be emotionally supportive that are the most helpful. Those compassionate efforts should receive attention equal to efforts to stop a bullying situation that may not be, practically speaking, entirely stoppable.

Notes

1. Mendez, L.M.R. and Knoff, H.M. (2003). Who gets suspended from school and why: a demographic analysis of schools and disciplinary infractions in a large school district. *Education and Treatment of Children* 26 (1): 30–51.

2. American Psychological Association Zero Tolerance Task Force (2008). Are zero tolerance policies effective in the schools? An evidentiary review and recommendations. *American Psychologist* 63 (9): 852–862. https://doi.org/10.1037/0003-066X.63.9.852.

3. Ibid.

Chapter 21
Myth #20
When kids shake hands and make up, the bullying stops.

T he documentary film *Bully* tells a powerful story about a chronically harassed and profoundly socially isolated boy. One of the most memorable scenes in the movie is when a bully, under duress by an administrator who's hovering nearby, agrees to offer his target a handshake. The victim very reluctantly complies with the gesture, afterward pointing out that the bully didn't really mean it. The administrator tells him, "By not shaking his hand, you're *just like him*" (emphasis added). The victim retorts, "But I don't hurt people." The scene is astonishing not because the adult is uncaring – she's evidently doing her best – but because she seems completely unaware of the power imbalance between bully and victim and of her

25 Myths About Bullying and Cyberbullying, First Edition.
Elizabeth K. Englander.
© 2020 John Wiley & Sons, Inc. Published 2020 by John Wiley & Sons, Inc.

own actions that effectively blame the victim. Adults may sometimes be unmindful that a more powerful bully is not really motivated to reconcile with a victim, but targets of bullying are rarely unaware of this. It's not hard to see how a bully might only pretend to comply. What makes this all somewhat confusing is that shaking hands is obviously very appropriate in many situations, especially when kids fight; it's an example of reconciliation, and there's a growing movement that emphasizes the value of conciliatory measures as the best way to respond to some types of interpersonal aggression. Part of that renewed emphasis on trying to make it right is the recognition that apologies and reconciliation can be very healing.

In recognition of this, schools may use mediation techniques to encourage kids to apologize and reconcile. But for mediation or reconciliation to be successful, the aggressor needs to be genuinely sorry, to express that regret, and the target must be able to trust him and believe him. Sometimes, of course, both parties are aggressors, as in a fight. In those situations, if both kids want the problem to end, then mediation and apology can work very well. Indeed, teaching kids how to mediate problems, find a solution, and apologize for the hurt they've caused is a way of teaching and reinforcing incredibly valuable life skills. This set of social skills will help kids retain their most valuable relationships and strengthen them, so you might think it would also be the best way to address bullying. But unfortunately, mediation doesn't appear to work in bullying situations: almost two-thirds (63%) of the subjects I studied in 2018 said that the most common way adults "make bullying worse" is by forcing a bully and a target into a mediation.

I think the reason mediation and apologies often are not effective in bullying situations has to do with the circumstances that must be present before mediation can work. Most notably, all involved parties have to really want the problem (i.e. the bullying) to stop. While a target clearly wants that, the bully is usually quite content to be on top socially and typically has no motivation to end the bullying. Second, the aggressor (or the bully) has to acknowledge that what they did was wrong and hurtful, and not justifiable or excusable. In my study of almost 600 teens in 2018, 60% of kids who admitted to bullying others felt that, in retrospect, their behavior was justifiable and understandable. That kind of attitude would make any apology or mediation futile.

Finally, for an apology and reconciliation to work, everyone has to be truthful and genuine. But while we all like to think that kids would never lie to us, the fact is that lying among children and teens isn't rare or even necessarily a sign that something's terribly wrong. Kids can be very convincing liars; and although adults often believe they can tell when a lie is being told, we're not as skilled at picking up on a falsehood as we think. In 2017, a group of researchers combed through 45 different experiments, all testing the idea that adults can tell when children lie. Overall, they found that the 8000 adults studied could see through a child's fib only 47.5% of the time.[1] None of us can *always* be in the half that can tell when a child is stretching the truth.

So while apologies and handshakes after bullying seem, theoretically, like a good idea, and the bully may appear to be genuinely asking for forgiveness, in reality, unless everyone's invested and truthful and acknowledges their wrongdoing, the effort is going to fall flat. Or worse – it may be interpreted as a veiled threat: *I may be doing what this adult wants me to do, but you and I both know that I'm going to get you back for this when everyone's back is turned.* None of this is to say that apologies for bullying will never work. But I've seen very few incidents where they have.

To-Do for Myth #20: When kids shake hands and make up, the bullying stops.

While mediation and apologies sound good to adults, kids are understandably wary. Adults should never force or compel kids to engage in mediation, and they should understand

(*continued*)

(*continued*)

that an apology may actually imply a threat of retaliation to a bullying victim.

The best strategy, on the whole, is to try to figure out if a problem is more like a fight (equal power, both kids being aggressive) or more like bullying (unequal power, one kid being aggressive, the other a target). If a situation seems more like a fight, it's probably more appropriate to pursue the idea of apologies and mediation. If it seems likely to be a bullying situation, apologies may not work.

Note

1. Gongola, J., Scurich, N., and Quas, J.A. (2017). Detecting deception in children: a meta-analysis. *Law and Human Behavior* 41 (1): 44–54.

Chapter 22
Myth #21
There's no point in forcing kids to be nicer to each other, because they'll just be mean again when the adults aren't there.

L et's be clear: sibling rivalry and some smarminess between siblings and friends are normal. A family joke recounts a time when I picked up my youngest toddler to cuddle him; he looked back at his older siblings and smirked, drawing a finger across his throat. *I got her this time*, the gesture said. *Try to displace me, and you'll incur her wrath. Nyah nyah nyah.*

25 Myths About Bullying and Cyberbullying, First Edition.
Elizabeth K. Englander.
© 2020 John Wiley & Sons, Inc. Published 2020 by John Wiley & Sons, Inc.

In the same vein, it's reasonable to assume that all kids use language when they're alone together that they would never use in front of adults. You probably remember the thrill of using swear words you were forbidden to use within earshot of any adult. Kids are good at compartmentalizing; they know better than to call each other *butthead* (or worse) or to throw around threats toward each other in front of Dad or the teacher. Again – this isn't pathology; it's a normal part of being a kid. In fact, maintaining a corner of their world where only children are in on the jokes and part of the power structure is an essential part of growing up. Using forbidden language is a relatively safe way of testing the limits and stretching your wings.

So, it's rational to ask, what's the point of making kids use decent language with each other and insisting that they *not* rake their nails across each other in the backseat of the car? If you know there will be pockets of time without adult supervision, why bother to put forward rules that will only work when adults are present? Should you bother to insist that your children not call each names when you know they might do it the moment you walk out of the room? Without interfering with the normal process of growing up (and you won't, you couldn't, even if you tried), there are three good reasons to enforce civility when you're within earshot. All three of these reasons influence a child's tendency to bully and to tolerate bullying.

The first reason is about teaching your child your values. Parental rules aren't only worthwhile if they're able to be enforced 24/7; they also have value as a way of teaching your child what you think is right or wrong. If you tell your child that the rules say they cannot hit, then you're teaching them that hitting is immoral. Chances are, you've told your child that they should not hit others, or cheat, or steal, or lie. They may still do these things when you're not around; but they'll know they're not supposed to, and doing something that you know is wrong is a very different feeling than doing something that you believe there are no rules about. Consider a child whose parents tell him that he shouldn't drink until he's of legal age, and compare him with a boy whose parents never bring up the issue. Both boys may drink at a high school party, but the first will feel some reservations and may limit his drinking, while the second likely won't give it another thought. As your child's parent, what you think is right or wrong is powerful and influences what your child thinks and feels; if you believe that treating others civilly and considerately is key, then expressing this belief is an important parenting habit. Many parents I've discussed this with have the sense that they may not need to openly discuss being nice, considerate, kind, or civil, as long as they set a good example. That's not wrong, but laying down what you believe frankly (and verbally) is always a good idea – and, interestingly, I've worked with many kids who weren't quite sure what their parents thought about bullying. You want your child to know *exactly* what you think about it.

The second reason it's a good idea to set rules about considerate behavior toward others is that even among nice kids, bad language and smarminess can very easily become a habit. A mom once wrote to ask me about how her son berated and put down his little sister every day: it wasn't about a fight or disagreement anymore; it was just a habit. He came home, went looking for his sister, and vented any frustrations he may have had that day in her direction. Plenty of siblings get into the habit of name-calling (in a more mean-spirited way), and that can also begin to have nothing to do with any conflict or problem per se. Letting this type of behavior go unchecked can help such a pattern form. On the other hand, setting expectations for civil language will ensure that your kids will watch themselves at least some of the time; and that alone can help prevent knee-jerk language from turning into a habit.

The third reason for enforcing civility and consideration is an issue that is especially important for siblings. The way brothers and sisters treat each other while growing up can influence their emotional impressions of their relationship, possibly for many years to come. What I'm referring to here is the general feeling siblings have about each other. Does their brother or sister hate them or like them? Do they have fun together, at least sometimes? Do they support each other in times of stress? Occasional fights, spats, and name-calling don't impact a relationship much; but a constant, unchecked barrage of abusive language takes its toll. Siblings whose only memories of each other focus mostly on negative, nasty interactions are much less likely to form strong relationships later in life.[1] The more you let your kids freely put each other down, the less they'll feel generally positively about each other.

The practical problem, of course, is what to do if you have two kids who constantly snipe at each other. The prospect of having to jump down their throats every 10 minutes is understandably too much to contemplate. Every parent knows to pick and choose their battles. But Mother Nature has already come up with a solution. No parent could take having to actively enforce every single rule, all the time. Thankfully, children abide by most of our rules without our having to actively compel them. Once your kids know the rules about being civil and considerate, and once they know you will enforce those rules when you see them being broken, they're much more likely to behave without you needing to be a constant disciplinarian.

What's more, these rules about how your family members should treat each other have a lot to do with bullying and with the odds that your children will become involved, especially as a bully. In my research, when bullying happened between siblings, those siblings were much less likely to view cruel behavior with peers as clearly wrong. In addition, these kids were almost four times more likely to view most people in high school as mean. It may be that bullying between siblings actually worsens a kid's outlook.

So letting kids be mean and abusive toward each other on a consistent basis seems to have consequences that include, but even go beyond, family life. It may be that failing to respond to sustained meanness between siblings teaches your kids that cruelty is a normal fact of life that they'd better accept. If your goal is to raise a child who's not a bully, then sensitizing them to how they make other people feel is a great place to start.

To-Do for Myth #21: There's no point in forcing kids to be nicer to each other, because they'll just be mean again when the adults aren't there.

Don't be afraid to tell your kids what you think is right or wrong, especially when it comes to how they treat other people. And this isn't likely to be a one-time conversation; rather, it is an important thread that runs through everyone's life. It might make you feel geeky or old-fashioned, but teaching your kids about the right way to behave toward their siblings and peers is one of the best ways to reinforce good behavior.

At the same time, don't realistically expect your children to be kind 100% of the time, especially toward each other. It's normal for siblings to run hot and cold: they might quarrel and shriek; and then, 15 minutes later, you'll find them playing together amicably. But having more one child still gives you regular opportunities to emphasize the importance of treating peers civilly. Those are opportunities you definitely don't want to squander.

Note

1. Lamb, M.E. and Sutton-Smith, B. (2014). Important variables in adult sibling relationships: a qualitative study. In *Sibling Relationships: Their Nature and Significance Across the Lifespan*. New York: Psychology Press. https://doi.org/10.4324/9781315802787.

Chapter 23
Myth #22
If only kids would report to adults, the problem would be solved.

Whenour kids have problems, we want to hear about them; and you may feel that's never truer than when it comes to bullying. The problem is what to do with the information. On the one hand, most parents clearly want to know when their child is hurting; but on the other hand, many also feel helpless when a child is being bullied, and aren't sure what to do or how to respond. In addition, most adults are uncomfortably aware that aggressively intervening could make things worse. In my 2018 study of 867 teens, almost a third of bullying victims said that reporting resulted in the bully taking revenge, predominately (but not only) online. Trying to resolve a bullying situation can easily have

25 Myths About Bullying and Cyberbullying, First Edition.
Elizabeth K. Englander.
© 2020 John Wiley & Sons, Inc. Published 2020 by John Wiley & Sons, Inc.

unintended consequences; it can lead to retaliation, either by the bully or by his or her friends; it can escalate a situation, especially online; or it can worsen or lengthen an incident that might otherwise have resolved itself more quickly.

Despite those realities, you've probably heard the relentless drumbeat emphasizing the central and critical importance of reporting. Kids are typically told little else about bullying, in fact; strategies beyond simply reporting to adults sometimes aren't even explored. All of this ignores several central facts. First, despite adult encouragement to report, the kid-enforced ban on running to adults can be so strong and iron-clad that it's unusual for targets of bullying to violate it. Second, there's a good reason to question whether telling adults is *always* the very best strategy (especially when it's the *only* strategy that's used). Finally, the value of talking to adults may not be in the actions they take, but rather in the emotional support they can offer. The Youth Voice Project's research found that listening to kids, checking in with them, and giving them advice were the most appreciated adult responses to a child's report of bullying.[1] In my 2018 research, the results were the same. Kids told us that the most helpful actions adults take are supportive, rather than action-oriented. Approaches like putting the target and the bully in mediation, or having an adult ask other kids to support the target, were rated as least helpful.

It's also important to remember that not all adults are alike; and to a child, their parents and their teachers or educators play very different roles in their lives. In my research, kids are far more likely to report to parents, for example, than they are to report to school adults. That makes sense. The relationship counts, and it's normal for kids to prefer to talk with their mom or dad.

Of course, kids don't always want to talk to adults – when it comes to social problems, there are many circumstances where they might prefer to talk to friends and peers. And that's not a bad strategy when you're being bullied. In my research, kids who were targets of bullying or cyberbullying reported that peers were more responsive to their social problems than adults were. For example, 82% of targets said a peer followed up after a bullying report, while 65% said an adult checked back in with them. More than one-third (35%) of the time, adults *never* got back to a child who reported being bullied. When I asked targets of bullying whether it was helpful to report, 71% said reporting to peers was helpful, but only 24% said that telling an adult definitely made a difference.

I wouldn't want these statistics to be misinterpreted as demonstrating that kids find talking to adults pointless or useless. Actually, reporting to adults was often rated as useful – but not in the way most adults envision. Grownups often think of reporting as the first step in taking action in a bullying situation; but targets tend to view an adult's best role as a source of emotional support, rather than as a strategic advocate who will quickly and definitively stop a bullying situation. When targets of bullying were asked in 2018 which adult actions are most helpful, the two top answers were "They check in with you frequently" and "They talk to you and are supportive, even when they can't stop the bullying." In contrast, only 5% of targets felt that having the bully and victim sit down together and try to "work it out" was helpful; and only 7 and 7.3%, respectively, felt that reprimanding or punishing the bully was ultimately helpful.

Peer support is powerful; in the social world of kids, it's a power that we should never disregard or ignore. Telling kids it doesn't matter what their peers think of them, or that they shouldn't care what anyone else thinks, isn't likely to be well-received or helpful. In schools and online communities, kids have the most power to make their peers feel either terrible or wonderful. In a bullying situation, peer support can literally transform the experience for a target. This isn't to say that adult support doesn't also have an important role. Of course, it's up to adults to assess whether something truly damaging, threatening, or dangerous is occurring. But grownups can also provide emotional support that can be critically important, especially for kids who struggle to make friends. Encouraging kids to consider *all* strategies (including emotional support) and to talk with everyone who cares about them – friends, siblings, teachers, and parents – seems like a sensible message.

To-Do for Myth #22: If only kids would report to adults, the problem would be solved.

There are two main takeaways from this chapter. First, understand that your child's friends and peers play a very important role in helping them cope with bullying and cyberbullying. Second, appreciate that your role may not always involve leaping immediately to strategic responses; you can help respond, of course, but you are also a key source of emotional support, and that may be what your children really want from you during difficult social conflicts.

Reporting to adults is very important in bullying situations, but it isn't the only strategy and shouldn't be promoted as the be-all and end-all of resolving such problems. Kids can and should be encouraged to seek out the help and attention of friends when they are being targeted by a bully. Other peers carry a great deal of weight and can potentially be very healing in a bullying situation.

This doesn't mean parents shouldn't encourage their children to report bullying or cyberbullying when they occur. Encouraging children to talk to family (including parents) is a habit that can serve kids well their entire lives. But adults should always remember how important it is to provide emotional support: to talk and listen to victims of bullying. Going over strategies is always good; but even when you don't know what to do or what to say to help your child, just being there and caring counts for a great deal.

Note

1. Davis, S. and Nixon, C. (2010). The youth voice project. Pennsylvania State University. http://njbullying.org/documents/YVPMarch2010.pdf.

Chapter 24
Myth #23
The best way to stop bullying is for bystanders to confront bullies and stop bullying episodes.

There's a famous scene in the 1989 film *When Harry Met Sally* when Meg Ryan fakes an orgasm in the middle of a deli. In that scene, Billy Crystal states confidently that he's certain no woman has ever faked an orgasm with him. Ryan points out the bald truth: that "all men are sure it never happened to them, and most women at one time or another have done it, so you do the math." Sometimes we just don't like to confront an objective truth; we prefer to think that we're the exception to the rule, or that we somehow have better information than everyone else does. When both of these seem unlikely, people sometimes adopt other strategies when they're confronted with facts they don't want to believe.

25 Myths About Bullying and Cyberbullying, First Edition.
Elizabeth K. Englander.
© 2020 John Wiley & Sons, Inc. Published 2020 by John Wiley & Sons, Inc.

In the face of uncomfortable truths, we might reject the data ("Faking an orgasm is probably really rare, no matter what those statistics say"); alternatively, we might try to redefine the situation so we decide it doesn't apply to us ("Faking orgasms probably doesn't happen unless you've been with a partner for a long time").

The awkward ways we square how things are versus how we'd like them to be extends to bullying and our children, as well. A mother who admitted that her son was a bully justified the behavior to me by pointing out that the target had an annoying personal habit. She undoubtedly thought of herself as a mother who wouldn't raise an aggressive child; and to avoid the uncomfortable truth that her son was indeed bullying others, she redefined the situation as a justifiable reaction to an annoying peer. By the same token, many parents have confidently asserted to me that their child is one of the few who would readily and consistently step up and stop a bully. Yet we know that people who can confront aggressive offenders are rare. The truth is, confronting an aggressive person is an exceptionally difficult (and not always advisable) thing to do. Even adults have a hard time with confrontation when aggression or bullying is happening. Asking children to do it is a pretty tall order and might result in kids feeling like failures about their ability to address bullying effectively. In any case, most children don't confront. In a 2018 study of 867 teens in Massachusetts, Colorado, and Texas, I found that only 27% of targets said that someone confronted their bully in a way that helped them; that percentage dropped to 13% when the bullying was happening online.

Not only is actively and publicly confronting bullies exceptionally difficult, but it's also unlikely to help, and it may actually make things worse for the target. The Youth Voice Project found in their 2013 research that about 75% of the time, confronting a bully failed to improve a target's situation or made it worse.[1] Confronting a bully may make him or her feel that they're being publicly challenged or humiliated; and that, in turn, can motivate them to take revenge or to continue their campaign.

But if confrontation isn't a winning strategy, what do we say to the children who are able to be assertive? If we can find strategies that are effective and achievable, we can enhance children's sense of their own ability to address bullying. Both my research and others' have found that focusing on helping the target – instead of confronting the bully - can be very positive in several ways. First, we're encouraging kids to take action in a much more plausible way; it's easier to help than to confront someone. Also, we're encouraging kids to use a technique that doesn't involve giving an aggressive child their attention (which could inadvertently reinforce what the bully is doing). It's less risky for a bystander to help someone than to put themselves in the crosshairs of a bully. Finally, the approach of focusing on helping (versus reprimanding someone) is overall a much more positive and help-oriented intervention. It's the target who's the important person in this situation, and they should get the focus and support of others.

To-Do for Myth #23: The best way to stop bullying is for bystanders to confront bullies and stop bullying episodes.

Strength and resiliency are prized characteristics in our society. This can be especially true for boys, but it's true for girls as well. However, fighting back isn't always the smartest strategy. When it comes to bullying, public confrontation appears to a risky approach. It can backfire; it can turn a well-intentioned bystander into another victim of a bully; it can heap public attention (if not praise) on a bully; and it can make life worse for a target. A smarter tactic might be to encourage kids to help each other when someone is being mean to them. It's not necessary to confront an aggressive

(*continued*)

(*continued*)

person; instead, they can help a target get away, or comfort them after the fact.

And it's not necessary to become a target's best friend or even to interact with them in depth in order to be helpful. I once conducted a study where I presented subjects with a scenario in which they were being publicly dressed down by a bully. A peer walked by and simply said, "Don't pay any attention to him!" Notably, 85% of the subjects said that just making that supportive statement was helpful. Apparently even recognizing that bullying is occurring and encouraging targets to disregard it is positive – especially when such statements come from other kids.

Note

1. Davis, S. and Nixon, C. (2010). The youth voice project. Pennsylvania State University. http://njbullying.org/documents/YVPMarch2010.pdf.

Chapter 25
Myth #24
The best way to deal with cyberbullying is to keep kids off their phones and computers.

I've felt this way myself. I walk into the living room, and there are the kids – all looking at screens. They're peering into their laptops or at their phones. And I think to myself, "If I was a good mother, I'd throw every one of those damned devices in the garbage and make the kids go outside."

There's some truth to this feeling. It's now a matter of common knowledge that kids spend too much time with screens and too little time on other types of interactions. The average American child today spends more than seven hours every day on screens – a number that may make any parent cringe.[1] By now, we've all heard about the issues that excessive screen time can contribute to: obesity, sleep problems, lack of physical exercise, poor social skills, even depression and anxiety. Anxiety tops the list of mental health problems associated with frequent screen use.[2] And not least of all is cyberbullying, and the very real possibility that your child will have digital encounters that damage their self-esteem, mental health, or social standing.

What to do? Sure, we could all just throw out everything that comes with a charger. But is it possible that your kids will *suffer* socially if they don't have their own device (i.e. a phone)? How do you tell your child that they can't play a game online that all their friends are playing? Isn't a lot of homework done online or on a computer today? What if their sports team or school activity posts information or other materials on social media? What if your child likes to do prosocial or educational things online, like reading books on a tablet or joining a social media group that contributes to charity? The truth is, the answer can't be simply pulling the plug. Still, the hazards of constant screen use are undeniable. So how can we juggle the good and the bad?

The first thing to realize is that kids aren't crazy. When they tell you they'll feel left out if they can't do what their friends are doing (e.g. playing a game online), they probably really will feel left out. Social events and get-togethers do happen online, and it's important for kids to feel included at least some of the time. Having said this, it is undeniably a part of life to occasionally feel left out, and you certainly don't have to let your kids run roughshod over you with their digital requests. It's likely that your parents didn't accede to all of your social requests. If your kids generally get to play online with their friends, then saying "no" now and then isn't likely to cause any serious problems, and it may be good for them.

The second thing to realize is that as kids go through adolescence, they tend to better understand the importance of balancing technology use with other activities. As teens get past early adolescence, many begin to develop a sense that constant screen use is not attractive or smart. Of course, there's a lot of individual variation; but the total and utter screen absorption that characterizes so much of middle school and early high school does seem to wane in a few years. In a focus group I once ran with college students, many derided the kids who constantly had a phone in their face. I heard statements like, "They're missing out on real life" and "They can't focus on anything or anybody else."

The third thing that can be helpful to keep in mind is that complete avoidance of technology probably isn't a good strategy. Our children will be using technology and social media all their lives: in their personal relationships, during work, at school, and for planning, travel, shopping, etc. Indeed, you may be using digital technology for all those purposes yourself. You may be reading this book on a screen; I'm certainly writing it on a screen. So practice with digital communications is important, because usage is inevitable. And giving your kids some guidance about *how* to use technology is almost certainly a better approach than simply avoiding it.

Finally: *of course* your instinct is correct – your kids do need time for traditional social interactions, away from screens. They need to be around a variety of activities and people. Those experiences can help your child develop social skills, connect with others meaningfully, and pay attention to their world in a way that they might not otherwise. It may surprise (or please) you to hear that in a 2017 study at the Massachusetts Aggression Reduction Center, I found that 86% of teens felt that overall, technology does not make for stronger and closer interpersonal relationships. Time away from screens, and the stronger relationships that can result, can help kids cope better if someone does try to bully or cyberbully them. Schedule family time without screens, like dinnertime together, Sunday walks in the woods, or family game time (with traditional board games). Your kids may resist initially; but in the long run, they are likely to come to see these times as fun in a different way!

To-Do for Myth #24: The best way to deal with cyberbullying is to keep kids off their phones and computers.

Guided use of social media and apps is probably the answer, with scheduled and regular screen breaks. By this I don't mean constantly peering over your child's shoulder, but instead, having conversations about how digital technology use is going these days. You might ask things like:

> "What games or apps are you and your friends using most these days?"

> "I know that comment makes you sound pretty clever! But how do you think it'll make him/her feel when they read it?"

> "What do you think the rules should be about posting pics of other people? What would let you have some fun while still making sure you don't embarrass or hurt someone else?"

> "I've had experiences where I sent a message and the person didn't take it the way I meant it. Has that ever happened to you? What did you do to handle it?"

Notes

1. Welch, A. (2019). Health experts say parents need to drastically cut kids' screen time. CBS News. https://www.cbsnews.com/news/parents-need-to-drastically-cut-kids-screen-time-devices-american-heart-association/.

2. Jiang, J. (2018). How teens and parents navigate screen time and device distractions. Pew Research Center: Internet & Technology. https://www.pewresearch.org/internet/2018/08/22/how-teens-and-parents-navigate-screen-time-and-device-distractions.

Chapter 26

Myth #25
Just ignore them, and they'll leave you alone. That's the best strategy for dealing with bullies.

Ignoring bullies is a common piece of advice; in fact, in my own research, it's the advice that kids get most frequently from adults. But if you've ever seen the misery on the face of a child who's being repeatedly mocked, excluded, made fun of, or put down, it's not too tough to see how hard it can be to take this advice to heart. In reality, ignoring bullies can be very difficult. Social cruelty isn't just a random, unpleasant event; when you're a kid in school, social cruelty is also a challenge. Adults may coach their children to "not care what other kids think"; but in reality, youth are strongly motivated to care what their peers think, because caring how you appear to others, and being motivated by what others

25 Myths About Bullying and Cyberbullying, First Edition.
Elizabeth K. Englander.
© 2020 John Wiley & Sons, Inc. Published 2020 by John Wiley & Sons, Inc.

think of you, is a major way we all become socially connected. As we get older, we learn to sift apart the opinions of those whose judgment we really value (for example, family) from those whose judgment we don't care much about (for example, strangers). But children haven't yet learned to do this well, so the words and actions of a bully can cut to the quick, regardless of whether that child is their friend.

When bullying goes online, ignoring a bully can seem even harder for kids. Celia Brown, a graduate student in Connecticut, conducting research on the impact of social media, pointed out how online, teens (and younger kids) can experience a heightened feeling of an "imaginary audience." *Imaginary audience* is the sense adolescents have that everyone else is scrutinizing them constantly; this skewed impression of how interested others are in you is a normal part of growing up, and it accounts for the intense need teenagers have for occasional privacy (escaping the ever-present scrutiny) and their overreaction to small physical imperfections. But while a sense of imaginary audience is normal for teens, this feeling can be expanded for kids of all ages by the use of social media. When a user is on social media, they are both messaging others and posting information and pictures. But Brown points out that one of the key elements of social media is the fact that any given user often has no actual information about how many people view what they post; and this lack of knowledge tends to inflate the estimates that many make about how large their "imaginary" audience is.[1] Maybe only one kid from your school saw that picture, but you may believe that 100 did. It's not hard to imagine how the sense that "many" people are watching online could decrease someone's ability to "just ignore" digital forms of bullying.

Despite the fact that ignoring bullying is easy to recommend but not, apparently, easy to accomplish, adults often advise kids to do just that. With certain types of bullying, common sense dictates that indifference won't have an impact. For example, there's no obvious way to ignore physical bullying; and in a digital environment, no one may know if a target is ignoring bullying (although they may notice if he or she responds). In addition, even if kids can ignore psychological bullying that happens in person, such an approach isn't usually effective in improving the situation, according to research that examines how well different responses work. A few years ago, I asked kids what kinds of strategies adults advised them to adopt when they reported being bullied. Overwhelmingly, the adults tended to recommend two strategies: ignore the bully, or simply decide the bullying isn't a problem because the bully has no real power over you. These weren't rated as effective strategies in the research conducted by Stan Davis and Charisse Nixon at the Youth Voice Project. In that study, which asked 13,000 children the effectiveness of different approaches to bullying prevention and response, doing nothing or pretending the bullying didn't bother them were the strategies most likely to result in no change or the bullying getting worse. In the field, I've noticed several cases where trying to ignore bullies resulted in the situation escalating to become significantly more threatening.

Yet despite all these issues, ignoring bullies can apparently work sometimes. What seems to be the key are the conditions under which the strategy is used. For example, in my research, adolescents report somewhat more success with ignoring bullies, compared to younger children. This may be because adolescents are better able to truly feign indifference; younger children are much more revealing and may struggle, when in the grip of their emotions, to keep a neutral face. But a target who convincingly appears completely indifferent and unbothered by a bully may be given up on fairly quickly. In addition, combining advice to ignore bullying with social support might render it more helpful.

I conducted an experiment that tested this idea. Imagine that you're a kid again, back at school, in the hallway, perhaps at your locker. Someone comes by: someone mean, perhaps a bully. They start taunting you. "Where'd you get that sweater?" they ask. "From your blind mother, who made you wear it? It's the ugliest thing I've ever seen!" (This is accompanied, of course, by raucous laughter.) But then someone else walks by. He doesn't pause; he doesn't touch you; he doesn't even know you. But as he passes, he looks at you and says – loudly – "Don't pay any attention to him. He's a jerk."

Would just a remark, essentially encouraging you to ignore a bully, make you feel better? Possibly; but especially if that sympathetic passerby was another student. In this experiment, the only element I varied was the identity of the passerby. Half the time it was an adult, and half the time it was another student (a peer) who walked past. Next, I asked if it seemed helpful when the passerby said that, and whether it made them feel better. When the passerby was an adult, 29% of the youth we studied said the remark made them feel much better; but when the passerby was another youth, that percentage rocketed up to 85%.

All this might sound like a contradiction. On the one hand, I'm saying that ignoring bullies doesn't work; but on the other hand, I'm also saying that in an experiment, peers essentially supporting kids in their efforts to ignore a bully was experienced as helpful. Both scenarios can be true; the key difference may be in *how* the message is delivered. If someone encourages you to ignore a bully, but they're not there to support you during the bullying, it seems to be a less helpful strategy. On the other hand, if you're in the middle of a bullying situation and someone makes eye contact with you and tells you the bully isn't worth paying attention to, then that's an active form of emotional support, and that situation seems to be more helpful for kids. As the Youth Voice Project stated, "Our students reported that *accessing support* from peers and adults was the most helpful strategy to make things better."[2]

All of this is consistent with the research that compares different strategies and how well they help targets of bullying feel better. Instead of focusing on the bully, targets who had the most success in dealing with bullying tended to focus on their social support systems. In the Youth Voice Project's 2010 research, the most successful strategies reported by targets of bullying were talking with adults or their friends. In my own research, I similarly found that targets of bullying reported that sticking close to their friends (playing with them, eating lunch with them, walking with them between classes, etc.) was the strategy that really helped them feel able to cope. But although the research has been very consistent in showing the helpfulness of support from family and friends, you might find yourself resisting this approach for a few reasons.

First, it's easy to fall into the mindset that it's the bully who should change, not the victim. From an idealistic point of view, that's completely correct; but reality gets in the way. The only person whose behavior we can control is ourselves. That's true for targets of bullying, it's true for parents of those targets, and it's true for school personnel. Even if we successfully craft a plan to change the behavior of a child who's engaging in bullying, that's not likely to be a fast adjustment, and children who are being targeted by a bully understandably want quick relief. Another practical problem with the fact that social support seems to uniformly help bullying targets is simply this: in my experience, these aren't strategies that adults tend to focus on. We often think about punitive strategies for the bully, despite the fact that these can badly backfire on a target. Or we suggest strategies that are exceptionally difficult, like confronting or ignoring a bully. But the research shows pretty clearly that these approaches are less likely to result in a child feeling better, more resilient, and more comfortable than trying to increase emotional and social support. What if we suggest to children that bullies aren't worth their attention, that the best strategy is to remind themselves that they have friends and family who love them and want to be with them, and that those opinions are the ones that count?

To-Do for Myth #25: Just ignore them, and they'll leave you alone. That's the best strategy for dealing with bullies.

Helping a child increase their social support is clearly a better strategy than advising them to ignore a bully. I pointed

(continued)

(*continued*)

out earlier that ignoring a bully might work in some circumstances; but backing up a child emotionally will always help, and it'll help with more than just the current bullying situation. If your child has good friends, that's a major asset for them socially. Unfortunately, making friends is all about social skills, which seem to be declining today, probably because of all the time our kids spend using screens (although there are other factors at play, too).[3] An amazing study that examined children who went away to a no-screens camp for less than a week found a big bump in their social skills after only five days without cell phones or computers.[4] When it comes to bullying (and to social relationships, for that matter), the strength of a child's social skills is increasingly seen as key. Some children seem to acquire social skills effortlessly, but for others, it's important to remember that social skills can be taught and learned.

Several researchers have looked at formal social skills programs conducted in schools, and their findings were that such programs do indeed help kids develop social skills, although not dramatically so.[5] But parents and families can also help children develop the social skills they need to make friends and thus shield themselves from the most severe bullying and cyberbullying.

There are three big ways that any parent can help youth feel more supported. First, parents can carve out important time for the family to be together and to have fun. Family time can be as simple as dinner, or it can be more elaborate, like holding a game night periodically or taking a hike. Family closeness is strongly related to mental health in children.[6]

The second issue that parents can help with is the development of social skills in their children. Human children will naturally connect with others, but the current generation

(*continued*)

of children is struggling more than previous generations to form relationships with their peers. I'm often asked why, and there are two obvious suspects: the challenges to social development posed by digital technology and social media; and the reduction in the amount of play children engage in, compared to previous generations. Make sure your kids have time and opportunities for free play. Encourage friendships, and if your children don't have friends at school, work with school personnel to identify opportunities to make friends there. Also think of activities outside of school where your kids can potentially make friends; and don't be afraid to seek professional help to assist your child in developing the social skills that can be so protective.

Finally, confirm that school personnel don't give out advice based on your child's personal characteristics or identity. In my research, one of the most damaging pieces of advice went to a minority of targets who were told by adults to change their own behavior to avoid bullying. For example, kids might be told to behave more conventionally, dress in a certain way, act less like another gender, etc. While possibly well-meant, such advice is a put-down and can be classic victim-blaming.

Notes

1. Brown, C. (2013). Are we becoming more socially awkward? An analysis of the relationship between technological communication use and social skills in college students. Connecticut College. https://digitalcommons.conncoll.edu/psychhp/40/.

2. Davis, S. and Nixon, C. (2010). The youth voice project. Pennsylvania State University. http://njbullying.org/documents/YVPMarch2010.pdf.

3. Giedd, J.N. (2012). The digital revolution and adolescent brain evolution. *The Journal of Adolescent Health: Official Publication of the Society for*

Adolescent Medicine 51 (2): 101–105. https://doi.org/10.1016/j.jadohealth.2012.06.002.

4. Uhls, Y.T. Michikyan, M., Morris, J. et al. (2014). Five days at outdoor education camp without screens improves preteen skills with nonverbal emotion cues. *Computers in Human Behavior* 39: 387–392. https://doi.org/10.1016/j.chb.2014.05.036.

5. Lo, Y., Loe, S.A., and Cartledge, G. (2002). The effects of social skills instruction on the social behaviors of students at risk for emotional or behavioral disorders. *Behavioral Disorders* 27 (4): 371–385. https://doi.org/10.1177/019874290202700409.

6. Thomas, P.A., Liu, H., and Umberson, D. (2017). Family relationships and well-being. *Innovation in Aging* 1 (3). https://doi.org/10.1093/geroni/igx025.

Conclusion
The Good, the Bad, and Why It Usually Isn't Ugly

For most people, going to the dentist isn't much fun; but it does improve your health, and we sit through it regularly because we know it's good for us. Routine, minor social cruelty or thoughtlessness is something like that. Some elements are frustrating, and occasionally they can become dangerous; but while social cruelty doesn't improve our health like a teeth cleaning, there are definitely optimistic facts about it to keep in mind. However, I'll begin here with what I find frustrating about social cruelty between children.

25 Myths About Bullying and Cyberbullying, First Edition.
Elizabeth K. Englander.
© 2020 John Wiley & Sons, Inc. Published 2020 by John Wiley & Sons, Inc.

The first thing I find difficult to swallow is how being a victim of bullying can actually change a person's thought patterns and feelings, at least temporarily. People who have been victims in the past are more likely to become victims again in the future, and they're also more likely to misinterpret neutral behaviors as bullying or abusive. I have a clear memory of a little boy telling me once about how his tennis partner was bullying him by lobbing the ball. He was sure the boy was doing it deliberately to vex him. I asked him, "Could it be that the other boy just wasn't a very good tennis player?" He admitted that he knew nothing about how skilled the other boy was at tennis, but still spoke about his "feeling." This sense that victims sometimes have, that bullying is everywhere, is a completely unfair consequence of what they've been through. After all, they've done nothing wrong, so why should they have to suffer these negative feelings? It's important to appreciate that this tendency, if not understood, can lead to adults becoming frustrated with children who see bullying in too many situations. Probably the best way to approach this is to gently point out to these children how there might be another way to view what happened ("I'm thinking that maybe he wasn't a very good tennis player, and maybe that was why he wasn't good at hitting the ball right to you.").

The second thing I think many of us find difficult to accept is the fact that sometimes bullies become people who are popular and successful. Bullies have become politicians, CEOs, doctors, lawyers, and even educators. In high school, they can be attractive, athletic, and popular. We would all like to think that life is ultimately just and evenhanded. But of course, it isn't always. Some bullies certainly find that their abusive behavior lands them in a lot of trouble or limits their opportunities significantly. But other bullies eventually learn the importance of improving how they treat others, or they learn to mask their behavior better.

The third issue that can be difficult to accept is that bullying and socially stressful situations don't always leave us with someone to blame. Being cruel to people can truly be accidental, although I very rarely see adults or kids who are able to accept this possibility. It's hard not to blame someone when you've been hurt. Of course, a situation where someone is being mean to somebody else accidentally isn't truly bullying, although it still can be very hurtful. True bullying isn't an accident; it's intentional, but that's not always simple to figure out. Suppose a child posts something hurtful but claims afterward that they didn't intend it to be texted around the school; we could still blame that child by saying "she should have known," but if she didn't realize that could happen, then she didn't realize it. Similarly, suppose a boy makes up a story about a target and tells it to two other boys; the story subsequently gets around the whole school, causing intense humiliation for the target. The "bully" *did* intend to hurt that boy's feelings, but not that much! In other cases, the harm done is completely accidental, even if it's truly harmful. This can happen, for example, because the aggressive child doesn't quite understand what they're doing. Online (as I pointed out earlier), accidental cruelty is even more likely to happen. I could post a photo of you that I don't mean for you to see or for anyone else to pass around, and yet both things can happen, and you can end up being terribly hurt even though that wasn't what I intended. Bullying can be a simple situation with a clear line of blame; but in many cases, that isn't so.

Finally, if your child has been the target of a bully, it's hard to keep in mind but important to remember that bullies are children who need our help. These children are engaging adults and other kids in a very dysfunctional way, but they're trying to signal that they need attention and intervention. For whatever reason, they don't know how to have strong and healthy relationships. These children need treatment and even some sympathy. Sometimes, it's helpful for a target to think about them that way (although not always).

Okay, now the rough stuff is done. I want to talk about a few important reasons for optimism. Bullying is a very upsetting topic and an upsetting situation, but it's important to keep some of the better facts in mind.

First, not all kids are significantly affected by bullying, and those who are may find themselves less and less affected as they grow. In my 2018 data, 20% of bullying targets felt completely unimpacted by bullying attempts; another 59% reported that bullying affected them less and less as the school year progressed. Bullying is not a life sentence. Without a doubt, friends help kids become more resilient. Also, many times when kids create new friends, begin a new activity, change schools, or go to college, that shift represents an opportunity for them to create a new social life. Today, the Internet also offers a different place for kids to socialize; and for some kids, that's extremely important and helpful. Children who can't find social support in person – for example, marginalized students – may find a strong and supportive community online.

Second, like all stressful experiences, social cruelty can sometimes help kids develop empathy for others. It's certainly not a method of self-improvement that anybody would opt for, but I've had several students who were victims of bullying. These kids became involved in bullying prevention work and research at my Center exactly because they wanted to help others, sometimes directly as a result of their own life experiences. I'm not suggesting that bullying improves all victims; it does not. Unfortunately, it can also lead to a target becoming more aggressive and acting out, rather than becoming more sympathetic and helpful toward others. But it's true that in many cases, kids are able to take this negative experience and in the long term turn it into a positive.

The third reason for optimism is that, as I've pointed out before, truly terrible outcomes are relatively rare in bullying situations. It's not that they can never happen, but they should definitely not be viewed as inevitable. Bullying usually is not a permanent element of anybody's life; and with help, support, coaching, and love, children who are bullied can get past these experiences and grow up to be wonderful adults.

You have an important role in your child's social life. Adults *can* learn to understand, address, and prevent bullying more effectively. Key skills are learning, first, to take the context of the mean behavior into account. Remember that it's not just what one kid does to another, but also the social context in which that child is operating. Don't just ask, "What did she do to you?" Instead, ask how things are going and what's happening socially with any child who wants to talk about social problems.

Second, adults can learn about and learn to identify gateway behaviors. Once you understand the form that bullying and fighting are most likely to take, any adult will be better at addressing these problems.

Finally, and perhaps most importantly, adults need to appreciate the critical role that emotional and social support play in helping kids develop healthy social relationships. Our connections to each other are what buffer us when our social existence becomes rocky. I can't think of a better skill for any child to learn than when it's a good time to turn to family and friends, and how to support them in turn.

Index

25 Myths About Bullying and Cyberbullying, First Edition.
Elizabeth K. Englander.
© 2020 John Wiley & Sons, Inc. Published 2020 by John Wiley & Sons, Inc.